DARING, DEADLY, BRILLIANT, BRAVE

HISTORY'S TOUGHEST PEOPLE

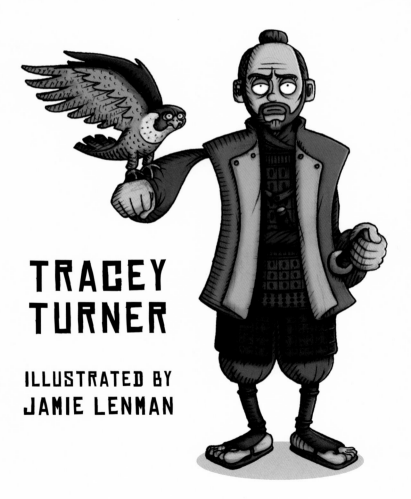

TRACEY TURNER

ILLUSTRATED BY JAMIE LENMAN

Sandy Creek
NEW YORK

For the two Ts

An Imprint of Sterling Publishing
387 Park Avenue South
New York, NY 10016

Copyright © 2012 by A & C Black
Text © 2012 by Tracey Turner
Illustrations © 2012 by Jamie Lenman

This 2013 edition published by Sandy Creek.

Picture acknowledgements: scrolls on pages 7, 10, 11, 41, 56, 101 all Shutterstock

ISBN 978-1-4351-4760-7

Manufactured in Shenzhen, China
Lot #:
2 4 6 8 10 9 7 5 3 1
03/13

CONTENTS

INTRODUCTION

This book contains some of history's toughest people, from fearless explorers to fearsome warriors. Some of them were peaceful (most of them weren't), many were extremely brave, and quite a lot were very violent indeed. But all of them were as tough as nails.

FIND OUT ABOUT . . .

- **Unstoppable conquerors**

- **Barbarian tribes**

- **The Way of the Warrior**

- **Vikings called Snake-in-the-Eye and Hairybreeches**

- **The Underground Railroad and the Trail of Tears**

If you've ever wanted to attend a terrifyingly tough Spartan boarding school, join the British Navy during the Napoleonic Wars, or fight in the ancient Roman gladiatorial arena, read on. Follow history's toughest to the freezing wastes of the South Pole, the bloody battlefields of the Civil War, and up the Ogooué River in Africa by canoe.

As well as discovering tales of bravery and cunning, you might be in for a few surprises. For example, did you know that Cleopatra married her little brothers? Or that ancient Roman leader Julius Caesar was captured by pirates?

You're about to meet some of the world's toughest people ever...

BATTLE OF THE TOUGHEST

Each of the people in this book has been given a *Tough Rating* and a *Toughometer* score for cunning, courage, survival skills, and ruthlessness.

Take the multiple-choice quiz on page 96 and find out how tough YOU are.

Create your pirate name on page 11.

Play the Exploration Game on page 62 and travel to uncharted territories.

BLACKBEARD

The notorious pirate Blackbeard gained his fearsome reputation in just two years. And he was *so tough* it seemed he was almost impossible to kill...

TOUGH
RATING: 7.8

BABY BLACKBEARD

We don't know much about Blackbeard's early life. He was born Edward Teach, probably in Bristol, England, around the year 1680. It is thought that Teach became a sailor in the Caribbean and the coast of North America during Queen Anne's War, fought between France and England. He most likely sailed on privateer ships, which were authorized by the government to attack foreign ships during a war, a bit like legal pirates.

PIRATE PARTNERS

After the war, Edward Teach joined the crew of a pirate called Benjamin Hornigold. He became Hornigold's second in command, and was put in charge of a ship of his own. Hornigold refused to attack British ships, which didn't go down well with his crew. He soon retired, while Teach went on to lead a life of crime on the high seas.

TOUGHOMETER

CUNNING: 8
COURAGE: 9
SURVIVAL SKILLS: 7
RUTHLESSNESS: 7

A REMARKABLE BEARD

Teach captured a French ship, and named it *Queen Anne's Revenge*. He became known as Blackbeard because of his long black beard, which he twisted into braids. The story goes that he stuck burning fuses into it and under his hat to make himself look as terrifying as possible.

AHOY THERE!

Blackbeard's reign of terror off the coast of Virginia and Carolina quickly became legendary. He captured lots of ships, gained a large fleet and crew, and gave himself the fancy title Commodore. In 1718 he blockaded the town of Charlestown and held its people to ransom. He wasn't very nice to his own crew, either—he shot his first mate in the knee during a drunken party.

PARDONED PIRATES

After two years of violence and thievery, Blackbeard accepted a royal pardon from King George I of England—which meant he wouldn't be caught and hanged, but he had to stop being a pirate. However, Blackbeard carried on plundering, and so the English Navy was sent to kill him.

BLACKBEARD'S GRUESOME END

The story goes that Blackbeard refused to die until he'd been shot five times and stabbed twenty times with a sword. His head was chopped off and hung from the bowsprit of the English ship. According to legend, Blackbeard's body swam around the ship before it sank.

YARR! COME ON THEN IF YOU THINK YOU'RE HARD ENOUGH!

HOW TO BE A PIRATE

Ahoy there! If you want to be a pirate, you'll need to be utterly ruthless, completely lacking in morals, handy with a cutlass, and motivated by greed. If that fits your description, read on . . .

TALK LIKE A PIRATE

Pirates have a vocabulary all of their own and you'll need to understand it if you plan on joining their ruthless ranks. Here are a few words to start you off:

Avast	Stop
Bilge	The lowest part of a ship inside the hull—can also be used to mean "nonsense" or "rubbish." Bilgewater is the foul water that collects in the bilge
Bilge rat	Insult (see above)
Booty	Loot
Cat o' nine tails	Whip made up of nine strands of rope
Fiddler's Green	Pirate heaven
Grog	Alcoholic drink (usually rum mixed with water)
Hearties	Friends
Hornswoggler	Cheat
Landlubber	Land lover—someone who isn't a sailor (can be used as an insult)
Jolly Roger	Pirate flag
Pieces of eight	Spanish silver coins
Sea dog	Experienced sailor
Shiver me timbers!	Surprised exclamation
Yarr!	Positive exclamation

YOUR PIRATE NAME

Simply choose any name from each of these three columns (or you could use your own first name instead of the middle column):

First Mate	Bart or Mary	Blackheart
Laughin'	Jack or Peggy	Diamond or Pearl or Ruby
Captain	Sam or Kate	Swagger
Jolly	Tom or Meg	Sharktooth
Peg-leg	Ben or Lizzie	Gold or Silver
Crazy	Pete or Annie	Hook

ACCESSORIZE!

Of course, if you really were a pirate, you'd need to dress like one! Here's how:

1. Grab a pair of canvas breeches, a shirt, a waistcoat, and a bandana to go round your head—the older and filthier the better.

2. Place all the clothing on the ground.

3. Chuck a bucket of seawater and half a bottle of rum over it. Leave to dry before wearing.

4. Accessorize with a parrot, a monkey, an eye patch, or large golden earrings. And, of course, a gleaming cutlass.

You're ready to terrorize the high seas!

GENGHIS KHAN

Genghis Khan united the tribes of the Mongolian Steppes and conquered one of the biggest and most impressive empires of all time.

TOUGH
RATING: 8.5

TEMUJIN

Genghis Khan was named Temujin when he was born in the Gobi desert, Mongolia, around 1162. His tribe was nomadic—the people roamed about with their horses and lived in tents. His father, the chief of the tribe, was poisoned and killed by a rival tribe when Temujin was just nine years old. Temujin's tribe didn't want a nine year old as their leader, so Temujin and his mother and brothers and sisters were abandoned to a life of poverty.

CAPTURED

It wasn't a good start. When he was a teenager, Temujin was captured by a rival tribe but managed a daring escape: a heavy wooden bar across his shoulders was supposed to stop him from moving, but he used it to bash his guard and broke free. The incident earned him a reputation for cunning and bravery. Soon afterward, he married the daughter of another tribal chief.

ONE BIG HAPPY FAMILY

With his new tribal alliance and his fearsome reputation, Temujin started to win followers. And it wasn't long before he began his conquering career. He began by uniting the Mongol tribes—there were lots of different ones, who were constantly fighting and plundering one another. Temujin gradually succeeded in uniting them, either by persuading them or bashing them into doing what he said. In one disloyal tribe he killed *everyone* except the children. By 1206, the Mongolian tribes were united, and Temujin was named Genghis Khan, which means "universal leader," the leader of them all.

MONGOLIAN HORDES

Genghis Khan created a disciplined, well equipped Mongol army. They were excellent riders, deadly accurate archers, and, it turned out, *really* good at conquering. Genghis and his Mongolian hordes rampaged into other parts of Central Asia, the north of China, Russia, and India.

ENORMOUS EMPIRE

By the time he died in 1227, Genghis Khan's empire stretched from Southeast Asia to Eastern Europe. Genghis was buried in an unmarked grave, as was the custom of his tribe. Legend has it that anyone unlucky enough to stumble across the funeral party was killed—so that Genghis's final resting place would forever remain a secret.

TOUGHOMETER

CUNNING: 8
COURAGE: 8
SURVIVAL SKILLS: 9
RUTHLESSNESS: 9

ENORMOUS EMPIRES

A whole lot of conquering has gone on during the course of human history. Here are the empires that conquered the most land.

1. THE BRITISH EMPIRE

Britain built settlements in many different parts of the world in the 17th and 18th centuries, to use as bases for trading goods. But most of the huge British Empire was gained during the reign of Queen Victoria. It was at its biggest around 1920, when Queen Victoria's grandson, George V, was in charge. The empire was spread out in different parts of the world—India, big chunks of Africa, Canada, Australia and New Zealand, and more besides. The empire ruled more than 450 million people, which was about a quarter of the population of the entire world at the time, and covered almost a quarter of the planet's land.

I WANT THIS BIT TOO!

QUEEN VICTORIA

2. THE MONGOL EMPIRE

Britain's Empire might have been the biggest, but the Mongol Empire, begun by Genghis Khan, was more impressive because it was one continuous chunk of land, not dotted around the world like the British Empire. Amazingly, it stretched all the way from the Pacific Ocean to the Mediterranean Sea. And it was gained by terrifying Mongolian hordes rampaging about on horseback. The Mongol Empire was at its biggest when Kublai Khan, Genghis Khan's grandson, was emperor.

3. THE RUSSIAN EMPIRE

The Russian Empire was vast—almost as big as the Mongol Empire. In the 1600s the Russians conquered Siberia, and by the end of the 19th century, the Russian Empire stretched from the Baltic Sea, up into the Arctic and across Siberia to the Pacific. At one time, Alaska was also part of the Russian Empire, but it was sold to America in 1867 for $7.2 million dollars, which worked out at around five dollars per square mile. The Russian Revolution put a stop to the expansion of the empire in 1917.

OTHER EMPIRES

The Roman Empire might have ruled most of the known world, but it comes quite a long way down the list of biggest empires ever: it was only a fifth of the size of the British Empire. The empire conquered by ancient Greek Alexander the Great was smaller still (although it was still pretty huge), about a fifth of the size of the Mongol Empire.

See page 46 to find out about Alexander the Great and his empire, page 50 to find out about Charlemagne and the Frankish Empire, and page 64 to find out about Aurangzeb and the Mughal Empire.

BOUDICCA

Boudicca was the queen of a British tribe in the first century AD. When the invading Romans turned ugly, she didn't take it lying down. Instead she stood up to the mighty Roman Army.

TOUGH
RATING: 7.5

BASHING BOUDICCA

Boudicca was the wife of King Prasutagus of the Iceni tribe in eastern England. Prasutagus got on well with the Romans, but when he died, in about AD 60, the Romans took the opportunity to grab the Iceni lands for themselves and treated the Iceni people very badly indeed. Boudicca herself was publicly whipped and beaten, and her daughters were attacked too. Despite the fact that the Romans were hugely powerful and ran most of the country, she decided to do something about it. She raised an army from her own tribe and a neighboring one, the Trinovantes, and led them in a revolt against the Romans.

BOUDICCA BASHES BACK

Boudicca headed for the Roman colony of Colchester, leading her army from her war chariot. Boudicca's army destroyed Colchester and defeated the Roman troops sent to fight them. Next Boudicca marched on to the trading settlement of London. The Roman governor, Suetonius, was in Wales when he heard about Boudicca's revolt. He took his troops to London, but decided to evacuate the settlement rather than stay and fight the fierce warrior queen. Boudicca's army smashed and burned as much as they could of London, then headed for St. Albans, a bit further north, where they did exactly the same thing.

TOUGHOMETER

CUNNING: 7
COURAGE: 9
SURVIVAL SKILLS: 7
RUTHLESSNESS: 7

THE BATTLE OF WATLING STREET

While Boudicca was busy in St. Albans, Suetonius
gathered his troops. Boudicca led her army to meet
them. The two sides met somewhere in the West
Midlands along the Roman road that's now called
Watling Street. The Romans began their assault on the
approaching British by launching thousands of javelins
at them. Then they advanced, pushing Boudicca's army
back so that they became hemmed in by the chariots
they'd left in a line at the edge of the battlefield.
Thousands were killed.

BOUDICCA'S END

Legend has it that Boudicca refused to be captured by
the Romans. Instead, she chose death, and poisoned
herself and her daughters using a toxic plant called
hemlock.

JOAN OF ARC

Joan of Arc was a French farm girl who never learned to read or write—yet she led the French Army and changed the course of history.

TOUGH
RATING: 7

ENGLISH VS FRENCH

Joan was born into a farming family around 1412 in a French village called Domrémy. Domrémy was divided by a river—one side was controlled by the Burgundians (English allies), and Joan's side belonged to supporters of Charles the Dauphin, who claimed the French throne. A war had been raging over who should be in charge of France since 1337!

VOICES

When she was about 13, Joan started having visions and hearing voices of various Christian saints (or that's what Joan believed). At first the voices just told her to be good, but later they told her to go to Charles the Dauphin's aid, get him crowned king, and drive the English and their supporters out of France! This was a bit of a challenge for a 13-year-old farmer's daughter, but Joan took it on.

SIR JOAN

Joan managed to get a meeting with Charles the Dauphin by being very stubborn and persuasive. After testing her to make sure she was on God's side, the Dauphin equipped Joan as a knight and sent her off to Orleans, a city besieged by the English.

TOUGHOMETER

CUNNING: 7
COURAGE: 9
SURVIVAL SKILLS: 5
RUTHLESSNESS: 7

VICTORIES...

Within ten days of Joan's arrival, Orleans was free from the English. Joan was a hero. She was put in joint charge of the French Army with the Duke of Alençon, and together they chased the English out of French towns, captured their castles, and outsmarted them in battle. Soon, Charles the Dauphin was crowned king of France at Rheims cathedral.

...AND DEFEAT

Joan had her first defeat when the French army tried to take Paris from English control. But worse was to come: in 1430 she was captured by the Burgundians. She was thrown into prison—and almost escaped twice—before being handed over to the English. A church court called the Inquisition questioned Joan for months. They found her guilty of being a witch and she was burned at the stake in 1431. Nearly 500 years later, the Catholic Church made her a saint.

SPARTACUS

Spartacus was a gladiator—a slave who fought other gladiators to entertain crowds of bloodthirsty ancient Romans. He managed to escape, raise an army of slaves, and lead them into battle against the fearsome Roman Army.

TOUGH RATING: 8

GLADIATOR SCHOOL

Spartacus was born around 109 BC, probably in Thrace (now Bulgaria). He was captured by the Romans and enslaved at a gladiatorial school near Capua, around 100 miles south of Rome. At the school they were taught how to fight one another to the death!

ESCAPE

In 73 BC Spartacus was part of an escape plot. Around 200 gladiators were about to make their getaway when they were betrayed, but they put up a fight. They made a run for the kitchens, armed themselves with anything dangerous they could lay their hands on, and took on the guards. About 70 of them managed to fight their way to freedom.

TOUGHOMETER

CUNNING: 9
COURAGE: 9
SURVIVAL SKILLS: 7
RUTHLESSNESS: 7

A CUNNING PLAN

Over the next few days the band of escaped gladiators was joined by more runaway slaves. They elected Spartacus and two other gladiators as their leaders and headed for Mount Vesuvius, where they were met by Roman troops. The Romans didn't realize that Spartacus and the slaves were busy making vines into ropes, abseiling down the other side of the mountain, and sneaking round to surprise them from behind. The Romans were defeated and Spartacus and his army marched on, defeating a second Roman force. They were joined by more rebels as they went.

ANGRY ROMANS

The rebels had divided into two forces, one led by Spartacus and one by Crixus. Crixus's 30,000-strong slave army was slaughtered by the Romans, but Spartacus's forces managed to defeat the Romans in revenge. By now the Romans were worried. The Roman general, Crassus, went after Spartacus and his rebels with eight legions (up to about 50,000 men).

THE END OF SPARTACUS

The rebel army managed to keep fighting for many more months. But eventually, in 71 BC, it was trapped in southern Italy and defeated by Crassus. Most of the slaves were killed. Spartacus's body was never found.

See page 22 for the Gladiatorial Games Survival Guide.

GLADIATORIAL GAMES SURVIVAL GUIDE

Gladiators need to be ruthless, cunning, physically fit, and harder than a centurion's biceps. If a gladiator is going to last more than five minutes, he needs to know all about the different types of gladiator and their weapons.

THE HOPLOMACHUS is dressed to look like a Greek Hoplite soldier and is often pitted against a Murmillo, similar to a Roman soldier, to represent Rome's glorious conquest of Greece. If you're a Hoplomachus you'll have a helmet and plenty of armor, and carry a spear and a short sword. But beware: if you're up against a Murmillo, the crowd will probably want the Murmillo to win (depending on where in the Roman Empire you're fighting).

THE MURMILLO has the short sword and shield of a Roman legionary (see above), and a helmet shaped like a fish. Depending on which Roman province you're in, the crowd will probably be on your side, as long as you put up a good fight.

THE THRAEX represents a Thracian soldier. With a small shield and sword, the Thraex can be at a bit of a disadvantage, especially since he has less armor than some of the other gladiators. If you're a Thraex up against a Hoplomachus, you're in for a tough fight.

THE RETIARIUS might feel a little self-conscious: he holds a net (which he can use to trap his opponent), a trident (think Neptune, god of the sea), and a dagger. If you're a Retiarius, you'll have some armor on your arms and legs but no helmet. However ridiculous you look, you're still expected to fight to the death.

THE WINNER TAKES IT ALL

Unfortunately for you, some gladiatorial contests are a fight to the death. If you lose but fight especially well you might be granted mercy—your opponent will be ordered to let you live, so you can fight another day. After a successful career as a gladiator, you might even be granted your freedom and escape the arena for ever.

WILLIAM WALLACE

William Wallace was a medieval Scottish rebel who refused to accept defeat. He became a Scottish hero and an English villain.

TOUGH
RATING: 8.5

ENGLISH SCOTLAND

Wallace was the son of a Scottish knight, but no one knows much about him until he was a young man. At the time, Scotland was under English control. Some of the Scottish nobles were imprisoned, and everyone had to pay taxes to King Edward I of England and fight in his wars if he told them to. In 1297, Wallace began a revolt by killing the English Sheriff of Lanark.

DO YOU HAVE THIS IN A SMALLER SIZE?

REVOLTING SCOTS

Supporters joined Wallace, who was good at giving rousing speeches, and they attacked the cities of Scone, Ancrum, and Dundee.

Another rebellious Scot, Andrew Moray, was busy fighting English control in the north of Scotland. The Scottish were soon back in charge of most of Scotland.

THE BATTLE OF STERLING BRIDGE

Wallace and Moray joined forces and together they faced the English Army at the Battle of Sterling Bridge. The English troops outnumbered the Scots but even so the English were battered and 5,000 of their men died, including Hugh Cressingham, an especially hated English noble. Legend says that Wallace had Cressingham's body skinned, and used it to make a gruesome belt for his sword. Moray was wounded and later died. Wallace was now Guardian of Scotland.

DEFEATED SCOTS

Wallace made raids into the north of England, but soon the Scots suffered a bad defeat at the Battle of Falkirk in 1298. Wallace resigned as Guardian of Scotland and probably went to France for a while to try and get French support.

NO SURRENDER

The Scottish leaders finally admitted defeat and accepted Edward I as overlord of Scotland in 1304. But Wallace refused. He was declared an outlaw, which meant anyone could kill him without punishment. In 1305 he was captured near Glasgow and sent to Westminster, where Edward I had him hanged, drawn, and quartered. To show what happened to rebels, different parts of his body were sent to Newcastle and various bits of Scotland, and his head was stuck on a pole on London Bridge.

TOUGHOMETER

CUNNING: 8
COURAGE: 9
SURVIVAL SKILLS: 8
RUTHLESSNESS: 9

HARRIET TUBMAN

Harriet Tubman escaped from a life of slavery in the United States. Despite huge risks, she fearlessly helped other slaves to freedom too.

TOUGH RATING: 8.3

A LIFE OF SLAVERY

Harriet was born in about 1820 on a plantation in Maryland. Like the rest of her family, she was a slave, hired out to work by her master from about the age of six. She looked after babies, set traps for pests, and later she worked as a maid and a farm laborer. She was often whipped and beaten by the people she worked for and bore the scars all her life.

TOUGHOMETER

CUNNING: 8
COURAGE: 9
SURVIVAL SKILLS: 9
RUTHLESSNESS: 7

ESCAPE!

In 1849, Harriet found out that she was going to be sold. After a failed attempt with two of her brothers, she escaped on her own. During the day she hid from the slave owners who would take her back to her master, where she would face serious punishment. She traveled at night using the Underground Railroad—a network of safe routes and hiding places, where there were people who helped runaway slaves. Eventually Harriet reached Philadelphia, Pennsylvania, where slavery had been abolished.

THE UNDERGROUND RAILROAD

Now a free woman, Harriet worked as a maid and saved her money, but not so that she could settle down. Instead, she put her life in danger again and again in order to help other runaway slaves. She acted as a "conductor," traveling on the Underground Railroad with escaped slaves and helping them to freedom, either in the northern United States or Canada. Runaways and those who helped them risked being re-enslaved, harsh punishments, and even death. Even though an enormous reward was offered for Harriet's capture, she was never caught. By the time the Civil War started she'd helped dozens—possibly hundreds—of runaway slaves, including her own parents and most of her brothers and sisters.

WAR WORK

During the Civil War, Harriet served as a nurse, a scout, and a spy for the Union Army in South Carolina. She was also part of a mission that sailed up the Combahee River to free hundreds of slaves from plantations in South Carolina. Slavery was finally abolished at the end of the war. Harriet settled in Auburn, New York, with her parents. She lived until 1913 and never stopped working for racial equality and women's rights.

See page 54 for more about the Civil War.

WILLIAM THE CONQUEROR

William was a Norman Duke who survived a perilous childhood, then conquered England when he grew up.

YOUNG WILLIAM

William's father died when William was about seven years old, making him Duke of Normandy. But life wasn't easy. Three of his guardians and his tutor were killed by rivals who wanted William out of the way, one of them in the room where William was sleeping. Once he'd managed to survive his childhood, he found himself having to deal with rebellions and fighting battles to crush them.

KINGS OF ENGLAND

William was keen for more land. His cousin, Edward the Confessor, King of England, had made him his heir (or so William said). But when Edward died in January 1066, the Saxon Harold Godwinson was crowned King Harold II of England.

INVASION!

William was furious. He gathered a mighty army and built hundreds of ships. The Normans landed at Pevensey on England's south coast and went on the rampage.

CUNNING: 9
COURAGE: 9
SURVIVAL SKILLS: 9
RUTHLESSNESS: 10

Meanwhile, King Harold had to sort out another invasion in the north of England before marching south to meet William. William defeated Harold's tired army at the long and bloody Battle of Hastings, where Harold was shot through the eye with an arrow and died.

THE BAYEUX TAPESTRY

A strange Norman fashion of the time was to shave the backs of their heads before battle. This hairstyle can be seen in the *Bayeux Tapestry*, a 70-yard-long embroidered record of the Battle of Hastings made in the 1070s.

WILLIAM GETS ANGRY

After the battle, William marched northward and began a terrible rampage around London, where he was crowned King on Christmas Day in 1066. The English rebelled in different parts of England but William managed to crush them all in the end. The biggest rebellion was in the north of England. William defeated the rebels then took his revenge: his troops killed people and animals and destroyed homes and crops, resulting in a terrible famine.

WILLIAM'S LAST REBELLION

In the end, the English rebellions stopped. The Normans took over English lands and Norman castles appeared all over the country. William was injured while destroying a rebellious French town in 1087, and died soon after.

NELSON

Horatio Nelson was a British naval officer who became the greatest hero of his time. Despite serious injuries he won dramatic battles at sea in the war with France.

TOUGH
RATING: 8

IN THE NAVY

Nelson was born in 1758. Following the example of his naval officer uncle, he joined the British Navy when he was just 12 years old. One of his early voyages was an expedition to the Arctic, where his ship became stuck in ice and Nelson chased a polar bear. Luckily for both bear and boy, Nelson didn't catch up with it. By the time he was twenty he was in command of his own ship.

EYE EYE, CAPTAIN

Nelson commanded ships in different parts of the world and rose through the ranks. During the war with Revolutionary France, Nelson lost most of the sight in his right eye defending the French port of Toulon, after sand and stones were blasted into his face during battle.

A SLIGHT SCRATCH

Nelson captured two enemy ships in his first big victory at the Battle of the Cape of St. Vincent. But not long afterwards, in another battle, he was hit in the right arm by a musket shot. The story goes that he refused to be helped aboard ship despite his shattered arm. He then demanded that the surgeon amputate it as soon as possible, and within half an hour he was back in command of his ship.

TOUGHOMETER

CUNNING: 8
COURAGE: 9
SURVIVAL SKILLS: 8
RUTHLESSNESS: 7

He recovered completely in time to defeat the French at the Battle of the Nile in Egypt a year later.

THE BATTLE OF TRAFALGAR

In 1805, the Emperor of France—Napoleon Bonaparte—raised a huge fleet of French and Spanish ships, determined to invade Britain. Nelson, by now a half-blind, one-armed Rear Admiral and tougher than ever, sailed to meet him at Cape Trafalgar with his own fleet, on his ship *HMS Victory*. Nelson's brilliant battle tactics won him his most famous victory of all. Napoleon's fleet, and his plans to invade, were left in ruins.

NELSON'S COLUMN

Nelson was shot through the spine during the battle and died of his wounds hours later aboard *HMS Victory*. His statue stands on top of Nelson's Column in Trafalgar Square in London, in memory of his greatest sea battle.

To find out more about life in the British Navy, see page 32.

IN THE NAVY

Congratulations! You've just joined the navy at the end of the 18th century, in the days of Lord Nelson and the Napoleonic Wars. You've got a lot to look forward to—seasickness, disgusting ship's rations, beatings, and extremely basic medical care.

ROTTEN RATIONS

Your weekly rations include rock-hard cheese, ship's biscuit (a kind of hard dried bread), salted meat, porridge, dried peas, and, if you're lucky, some pickled cabbage, and lemon or lime juice, which might stop you from getting scurvy. Scurvy is caused by a lack of vitamin C, and will make you weak, make your teeth drop out, and eventually kill you, so if there's any fresh fruit and vegetables to be had (there might be some at the beginning of the voyage), eat them. You'll also get lots of beer, and a drink of rum as a reward. Food, especially ship's biscuit, is often crawling with weevils and maggots.

BLOODY BATTLES

Battles are loud, terrifying, often very painful, and sometimes fatal. Your job is to load one of the cannons (preferably with proper ammunition, but if that's all gone anything you can find will do). You might also have to board an enemy ship, in which case there will be hand-to-hand fighting with cutlasses, pistols, axes, or anything else you can use as a weapon.

CRIME AND PUNISHMENT

If you're part of a mutiny (trying to get rid of an unpopular captain) or if you run away, the punishment is death. For other crimes—such as theft, being rude to an officer, falling asleep on duty, or being drunk—you'll be flogged on the back with a nine-stranded whip called a cat o' nine tails.

BOYS ONLY

Girls weren't allowed join the British Navy, but sometimes they disguised themselves as men and joined up anyway. Mary Ann Riley and Ann Hopping fought with Nelson at the Battle of the Nile, and Jane Townshend fought at the Battle of Trafalgar. Years later they asked Queen Victoria for medals, like the ones the male sailors had been given, but Queen Victoria refused!

To find out more about Napoleon Bonaparte, Nelson's French enemy, see page 78.

IVAN THE TERRIBLE

You don't end up with a name like that for nothing, and in Ivan's case killing thousands of people, including his own son, made him pretty terrible.

TOUGH
RATING: 7.5

IVAN THE INFANT

Ivan was born in 1530, the son of Grand Prince Vasily III of Moscow. His father died when Ivan was three, and Ivan became Grand Prince of Moscow. Since he was a bit young, his mom took over for him—until she died just five years later (possibly from poisoning). After that, nobles known as "boyars" struggled amongst themselves for power and treated Ivan very badly. But he managed to survive and hang on to his title, and when he was sixteen he was crowned Tsar of All the Russias, the first ever leader of the whole of Russia.

CONQUERING

Ivan changed the way the government was run, hoping to reduce the powers of the boyars and promote nobles who were loyal to him in their place. He also did a bit of conquering with some success, but wasted many troops and a lot of money fighting the Livonian War, which went on for 24 years without Ivan conquering anything.

TERRIBLE TIMES

Ivan was annoyed about the Livonian War and very angry indeed with some of the boyars, who had proved disloyal once again. So he gave himself special powers over particular areas of the country, formed a bodyguard (of about 1,000 men at first, but it grew much larger)

TOUGHOMETER

CUNNING: 7
COURAGE: 6
SURVIVAL SKILLS: 7
RUTHLESSNESS: 10

and began executing the boyars he didn't like, or who had plotted against him. He was especially suspicious of the nobles of the city of Novgorod, so he ordered his bodyguard to destroy it—they destroyed the whole city and killed thousands of people. Ivan the Terrible's reign of terror lasted seven years, during which he had at least 3,000 people executed.

IVAN JUNIOR

Ivan the Terrible's son and heir to the throne was also called Ivan. Unfortunately, in a violent fight, Ivan the Terrible killed Ivan junior by bashing him with a staff. Three years later, in 1584, Ivan died.

WU ZETIAN

Wu Zetian got rid of rivals, her husband, and even her own children to seize power for herself and become Empress of China.

YOUNG WU ZETIAN

Wu Zetian (also known as Wu Hou and Wu Zhao) was born in 624 into a fairly rich Chinese family. When she was 14 she was sent to the palace of Emperor Taizong to be his concubine—a sort of second-class wife (emperors had lots of concubines as well as a wife). When the emperor died in 649 she was sent to live in a Buddhist convent, along with the emperor's other concubines who didn't have children.

RIVALS

The new emperor was Taizong's son, Gaozong. His wife, Empress Wang, had a rival: Gaozong's favourite concubine, Consort Xiaou. Wang didn't want Xiaou taking her place, and thought that having the beautiful Wu Zetian at the palace might make things better. But her plan backfired. Wu Zetian quickly became Gaozong's favorite. Empress Wang and Consort Xiaou were both arrested, and Wu Zetian had them cruelly executed. Not long after, Wu Zetian was made Empress Wu.

EMPRESS WU TAKES CHARGE

TOUGHOMETER

CUNNING: 8
COURAGE: 8
SURVIVAL SKILLS: 9
RUTHLESSNESS: 9

Empress Wu also got rid of many senior politicians who didn't think she was good enough to be Empress of China. By 660 she'd managed to get them dismissed, sent into exile, or executed. Gaozong was unwell so Wu Zetian was able to rule in his place for the last 23 years of his life. Under her leadership, the

Chinese conquered Korea. But she was also ruthless: she had her son's wife starved to death and her parents exiled because she thought her husband favored the family too much.

UNSATISFACTORY EMPERORS

Gaozong died in 683 and Wu Zetian's son became emperor—but he disagreed publicly with his mother, and his wife was ambitious, so Empress Wu had them both sent into exile and made another of her sons emperor instead. She ruled in his place, and when a revolt took place she crushed it at once. In 690, she decided to do without an emperor altogether and took the throne herself. She ruled for fifteen years.

OF COURSE YOU'RE IN CHARGE, SON! YOU'RE DOING A VERY IMPORTANT JOB.

EMPRESS WU'S END

Finally Empress Wu became too old and sick to keep hold of her power. In 705, a group of generals and politicians executed her allies, and made the empress hand over power to one of her sons. She died five years later.

AMAZING ANCIENT CHINA

China is one of the world's oldest civilizations and so it has a very long and complicated history. To save time, here's the short version...

- People first lived in China tens of thousands of years ago, when people came to settle on the banks of the Yellow River.

- The Xia might have been the first Chinese dynasty—a powerful family that ruled the country—but historians can't agree whether they really existed or were just a story. After the Xia came the Shang—everyone agrees they really did exist (they developed writing) and ruled from about 1600 BC to 1046 BC. After them came the Zhou dynasty, who ruled for even longer.

- After the Zhou dynasty came a period known as the Warring States. During this time, tough guy Qin Shi Huangdi battled to unite China. Shi Huangdi managed to do so, became the first Chinese Emperor, and began the Qin dynasty. Imperial China lasted from the Qin dynasty to the end of the Qing dynasty in 1911.

- Dynasties came and went, and the Chinese territory split up into smaller bits then joined up again, and grew, shrank, and grew again. In 1271, China was part of the Mongol Empire under the Yuan dynasty, started by Kublai Khan, who built an enormous and beautiful palace in northern China that was big enough for 6,000 guests.

- A poor peasant, who became a Buddhist monk to avoid starvation, ended up overthrowing the ruling Mongols, as well as rival Chinese groups, and became the first Ming emperor. China started trading with other countries and grew wealthy. The Great Wall of China was built during the Ming dynasty.

- Invaders from the north conquered China, despite the Great Wall, and began the Qing dynasty, which lasted from 1644 to 1911. China's territory grew to its biggest ever size during this time.

- In 1911 the imperial court was overthrown and China was made a republic. In 1949 Communist leader Mao Zedong declared the People's Republic of China.

LIST OF CHINESE DYNASTIES

Xia 2700–1600 BC
Shang 1600–1046 BC
Western Zhou 1046–771 BC
Eastern Zhou 770–256 BC
Spring, Autumn, and Warring States Period 771–221 BC
Qin 221–206 BC
Western Han 206 BC–AD 9
Xin 9–23
Eastern Han 25–220
Three Kingdoms 220–265
Western Jin 265–317
Eastern Jin 317–420

Southern and Northern 420–589
Sui 581–618
Tang 618–907
Five Dynasties and Ten Kingdoms 907–960
Northern Song 960–1127
Southern Song 1127–1279
Liao 907–1125
Jin 1115–1234
Yuan 1271–1368
Ming 1368–1644
Qing 1644–1911

ATTILA THE HUN

Attila was a fierce warrior who led the most feared barbarian tribe of them all: the Huns. He helped finish off the Roman Empire forever.

TOUGH
RATING: 9

THE HUNS ARE COMING!

By the 400s, things weren't looking good for the Roman Empire. Some of the Romans' biggest problems came in the shape of ferocious barbarian tribes—among them the Huns, the most terrifying barbarians of the lot. They were horseback-riding nomads from Central Asia, fearsome warriors, and excellent archers.

HUNS VS ROMANS

Attila was born around AD 406. He and his brother Bleda became joint kings of the Huns in 434, when their uncle, the King of the Huns, died. By this time there was a huge Hun Empire. The Western Roman Empire had weakened and broken up. The stronger Eastern Roman Empire had its capital city in Constantinople (modern-day Istanbul). Attila and his brother demanded gold from the Romans—loads of it—in return for not destroying the Eastern Empire. But in the 440s the Huns attacked and conquered big chunks of the empire anyway. They stopped before attacking Constantinople, demanding even more gold from the Romans. By this time, Attila was the only king of the Huns: he'd had his brother murdered in 445.

TOUGHOMETER

CUNNING: 9
COURAGE: 8
SURVIVAL SKILLS: 9
RUTHLESSNESS: 10

A WEDDING PRESENT

Honoria, the Western Roman Emperor's sister, wrote to Attila asking him to get her out of an arranged marriage, and sent him a ring. Attila interpreted this as a proposal of marriage (which may or may not have been the case) and promptly demanded half of the Western Roman Empire as a dowry. When he didn't get it, he invaded Gaul. Honoria disappeared—she was probably murdered. The Romans joined forces with the Visigoths (a German tribe) and managed to drive the Huns out of Gaul, which made Attila very angry...

ATTILA STOPS RAMPAGING

In 452 Attila led the Huns on a rampage across the north of Italy, destroying the cities of Milan, Padua, and Verona, and lots more. The following year he had plans for further destruction, but something stopped him: he died. The story goes that he died of a nosebleed on his wedding night (Attila had lots of wives), but it's possible he was murdered.

Find out about Genghis Khan, leader of the Mongol tribes, on page 12.

THE BARBARIAN TRIBE GUIDE

From about AD 300, the Western Roman Empire began to fall apart, and there were plenty of barbarian tribes on the rampage helping it along. The Romans called anyone who came from outside the Roman Empire a barbarian, it didn't necessarily mean that they were brutal and uncivilized. Here's a quick guide to some of the different types.

HUNS

The Huns originally came from Central Asia, where they roamed about from place to place with their horses and other animals, and lived in tents. They were stocky, olive-skinned, and amazing horse-riders—children learned to ride as soon as they could walk. They fired arrows from horseback with deadly speed and accuracy. The Romans feared them more than any other barbarian tribe.

FRANKS

The tall, strong, mustache-wearing Franks came from the country we call Germany today. They used swords, lances, and throwing axes, not bothering with armor so that they could carry more weapons. They settled in what's now France, and gave the country its name.

SAXONS

The Saxons came from what's now Germany too. They expanded south and west, and became pirates in the North Sea. Some invaded

A FRANKISH WARRIOR

*LET'S BE FRIENDS

Britain, while others settled in northern Gaul (France), and had a long war with the Franks. In the end, the Franks defeated them under the Frankish leader Charlemagne.

GOTHS

The Goths came from what's now Scandinavia and Eastern Europe: the Ostrogoths (or eastern Goths) and the Visigoths (or western Goths). The Ostrogoths conquered most of Italy after the fall of the Roman Empire. The long-haired Visigoths settled in what's now southern France, until the Franks pushed them out.

WEIRD!

GOTHS ON THE WARPATH

VANDALS

The Vandals were driven out of their homeland in what's now Eastern Europe by the Huns and settled in Spain and North Africa. In 455 BC they destroyed and looted Rome (and, as a result, we still use the word "vandal" today). When the Romans fought back, the Vandals took 500 hostages on the Greek island of Zakynthos, chopped them to bits, and threw the pieces into the sea.

MARY KINGSLEY

Instead of staying at home with her embroidery like most other Victorian-era ladies of leisure, Mary Kingsley traveled to uncharted territories in Africa and had adventures with hippos.

TOUGH
RATING: 6

A QUIET LIFE

Mary Kingsley was born in London in 1862. Her father was a doctor who loved traveling—in fact he was seldom at home. He visited the South Seas, Africa, and the United States, where he narrowly missed a trip with General Custer to the Battle of Little Big Horn (Custer and his men were all killed there). Mary heard the stories of his adventures but was never allowed to go with him. She stayed at home, looking after the house, her brother, and her sick mother.

AFRICAN ADVENTURES

By the time Mary was 30 her parents were both dead. They'd left enough money to Mary and her brother so that they didn't need to work. Very few Victorian ladies would have chosen to travel, especially not alone, but Mary decided to change her life completely. She traveled first to the Canary Islands and then to Sierra Leone and Angola in West Africa. On her next trip to West Africa she visited Gabon, where she collected specimens of fish, insects, and plants for the British Museum in London. Mary traveled up the Ogooué River by canoe, through the country of the Fang people, who had a reputation for cannibalism, and became the first European woman to climb

TOUGHOMETER

CUNNING: 5
COURAGE: 9
SURVIVAL SKILLS: 8
RUTHLESSNESS: 2

Mount Cameroon. She claimed she had scratched a hippo behind the ear with her umbrella, and come close to being devoured by a crocodile. When she returned to England she published a book, *Travels in West Africa*, gave lectures about her experiences and wandered the streets of Kensington with a monkey on her shoulder.

LAST JOURNEY

Mary Kingsley had fallen in love with Africa. She went back for the last time in 1899, this time as a nurse for prisoners of war in the Boer War. The following year she caught the disease typhoid and died. Determined to be different, even in death, she was granted her wish to be buried at sea.

ALEXANDER THE GREAT

TOUGH RATING: 8.3

Alexander the Great was an unstoppable conqueror whose army was never defeated. His empire stretched from the Mediterranean to the Himalayas.

ALEXANDER THE TOUGHEST

Alexander was born in 356 BC in Macedonia, the son of King Philip II. Philip was powerful: most of Greece (to the south of Macedonia) was under his control. When Alexander became king in 336 after Philip was killed, he began his reign by killing his father's murderers and any rivals to his throne. Most Greek city-states were loyal to Alexander, but Thebes revolted. Alexander marched to Thebes, destroyed the city, killed thousands, and sold the survivors into slavery. Word spread that it wasn't a good idea to fall out with King Alexander.

CONQUERING

Persia had a nice big empire and Alexander had his eye on it. Along with some Greek allies, he crossed into Asia Minor (modern-day Turkey) and rampaged around the country battering the Persian army. Finally the Persian leader, Darius, ran away. Alexander marched south into Persian lands around the Mediterranean and Egypt, and soon he'd conquered the eastern Mediterranean coast.

EVEN MORE CONQUERING

Next on Alexander's list was Mesopotamia (modern-day Iraq). He met Darius's Persian army, complete with war elephants and chariots with scythes on the wheels, at the

TOUGHOMETER

CUNNING: 8
COURAGE: 8
SURVIVAL SKILLS: 8
RUTHLESSNESS: 9

Battle of Guagamela in 331 BC. Alexander won and was proclaimed King of Asia, while Darius was forced to run away *again*. Alexander next conquered Babylon and marched into Susa, the capital of Persia (modern-day Iran), collecting great hoards of treasure along the way.

JUST A BIT MORE CONQUERING

Alexander was determined to carry on eastwards. He marched into what's now Afghanistan, and on over the mountains into India, where he defeated the elephant-mounted army of King Poros. His army had had enough of conquering by this time, and reluctantly Alexander turned back. Back in Babylon, after a lot of partying, Alexander became ill and died. He was only 32 and he'd been King for just 12 years, yet he'd conquered most of the world—at least, the world he knew about—and founded dozens of cities, many of which are still called Alexandria today.

GANDHI

Gandhi got rid of British rule in India and changed the lives of millions of people. And, unlike lots of other tough people of history, he did it without bashing anybody.

TOUGH
RATING: 5.5

YOUNG GANDHI

Mohandas Gandhi was born in Porbandar, in the Gujarat region of India, in 1869. He trained as a lawyer in England, but when he came back to India there weren't many law jobs around. He took a job in Natal, South Africa instead.

UNFAIR LAWS

In South Africa, Gandhi was thrown out of train compartments, barred from hotels, and beaten up by a carriage driver—all because he was Indian rather than European (Natal was ruled by the British at the time). He decided to do something about it. He didn't find public speaking easy, but fueled by a fierce sense of injustice he organized other Indians against unfair laws—without using violence. Gandhi said there were many ways to react to injustice: you could put up with it, you could run away, you could fight using violence, or, the best and bravest way in Gandhi's view, you could fight it *without* using violence. He ended up in prison because of his organized protests, and so did hundreds of the people who followed him. Finally, he forced the South African government to agree to a compromise and release him and his followers from prison.

TOUGHOMETER

CUNNING: 5
COURAGE: 10
SURVIVAL SKILLS: 7
RUTHLESSNESS: 0

BRITISH INDIA

Gandhi came back to India

in 1914 and in just a few years, he became the most important politician in the country with millions of followers. India was still part of the British Empire, but Gandhi thought that India should be run by Indians. He led protests, and encouraged people to boycott British goods, courts of law, and schools. As a result, he was put in prison from 1922–24. When the British taxed salt in 1930, Gandhi led thousands of Indians on a 200-mile march to the sea to collect their own. He was sent to prison again, along with 60,000 of his followers.

INDEPENDENCE

Gandhi's way of changing things was peaceful but—eventually—just as powerful as if he'd had an army behind him. In 1947, India became independent from Britain. Gandhi had won his victory. He was trying to make peace between the two major religious groups in India, the Muslims and the Hindus, but, the following year, he was shot and killed.

CHARLEMAGNE

Charlemagne was a fierce medieval warrior king. The empire he founded lasted nearly a thousand years.

TOUGH
RATING: 8

PIPPIN THE SHORT

Charlemagne was born around 742. Ten or so years later, his father became King Pippin the Short of the Franks, the tribe that had fought the Romans hundreds of years before. The Franks had settled in Gaul (the country now called France, plus a few extra bits of neighboring countries).

TROUBLESOME SAXONS

When Pippin died in 768, Charlemagne and his brother Carloman ruled jointly until 771, when Carloman died and Charlemagne took control. He fought the kingdom of Saxony in what's now northern France, but it took him over *thirty years* of continual battles to defeat them. In 782 he ruthlessly killed 4,500 Saxon prisoners of war. When he finally won, in 804, he made the Saxons give up their pagan beliefs and become Christians.

TROUBLE IN ITALY

Meanwhile, back in 773, Pope Adrian I asked Charlemagne for help with the Lombards, who were causing trouble in Italy. Charlemagne sent his troops straight away and lost no time in thrashing them. Now he was King of the Lombards as well as King of the Franks.

CUNNING: 8
COURAGE: 8
SURVIVAL SKILLS: 8
RUTHLESSNESS: 8

CONQUERING

Charlemagne didn't stop there. He captured more land, in what's now part of Germany and Austria, converting people to Christianity as he went.

When he invaded Spain he was beaten by the Moorish (Muslim) Spanish rulers—which must have really annoyed him, because they weren't Christian.

RELIGIOUS EDUCATION

Charlemagne could speak several languages, and was a keen astronomer. He encouraged education, arts, and literature during his reign, but most schools were only for religious scholars. Despite his passion for learning, Charlemagne couldn't read or write, even though he tried very hard to learn.

THE HOLY ROMAN EMPIRE

In 800, Charlemagne saved Pope Leo III from an uprising. As a thank you, Leo proclaimed Charlemagne Emperor of the Romans on Christmas Day 800.

Charlemagne tried to make the Roman Empire as powerful as it had been before. The Holy Roman Empire, as it became known later, lasted almost a thousand years, until 1806.

Find out more about the Franks and other barbarian tribes on page 42.

ULYSSES S. GRANT

Ulysses S. Grant was an ordinary middle-aged store clerk, yet he led an enormous army to win the Civil War, and became President of the United States.

TOUGH
RATING: 8.3

YOUNG ULYSSES

Ulysses S. Grant was born in 1822 in Ohio, USA, the son of a tanner, and went to West Point Military Academy when he was 17. The United States was at war with Mexico when he left the academy, and Grant went straight into battle. He fought bravely and got promoted, but he didn't stay in the army for long. Two years after the war ended he left to return home to his wife.

CIVIL WAR

Grant tried farming and selling real estate, both of which failed, and finally he worked as a store clerk in his brother-in-law's leather business in Galena, Illinois. The Civil War began in 1861, fought between the northern states of America (the Union) and 11 southern states that had declared themselves independent (the Confederates). Grant began training volunteers for the Union Army. He seemed to have a knack for it. Before long, he'd turned a group of farm workers into well-disciplined soldiers and was made a brigadier general.

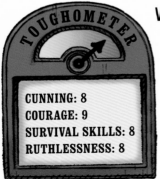

TOUGHOMETER

CUNNING: 8
COURAGE: 9
SURVIVAL SKILLS: 8
RUTHLESSNESS: 8

VOLUNTEERS

In 1862 Grant marched his army of 20,000 voluntary soldiers into Tennessee. They attacked and captured one Confederate fort, then besieged another. The Confederate general surrendered and Grant became a Union hero.

BLOODY BATTLES

Grant led the Union troops in the bloody Battle of Shiloh in Tennessee (one of the 11 southern US states). After two days of fighting, Grant won. The Confederate Army was pushed back and soon the whole of Tennessee was under Union control. Impressed with Grant's victories, President Lincoln made Grant "General in Chief," in charge of the entire Union Army. He went on to take control of the Confederate capital, Richmond, Virginia, and the Confederates surrendered.

GRANT THE HERO

Grant was showered with honors and gifts and became a national hero. Despite his complete lack of political experience, he was elected President of the United States twice, and enforced laws that meant African Americans were represented in Congress for the first time. After his second presidency, Grant went on a world tour, stopping off with royal families on the way. He died after writing his memoirs, which became a bestselling book.

THE CIVIL WAR
[THE SHORT VERSION]

The American colonies revolted against the British and gained independence in 1783, after a long war. Less than eighty years later the United States was at war again, but this time it was the North of the United States versus the South.

- Eleven southern states formed their own government in 1860, calling themselves the Confederate States of America. Their biggest disagreement with the rest of the United States was over slavery. In the South there were many huge farms called plantations, which relied on slave labor. The new president, Abraham Lincoln, seemed in favor of banning slavery completely.

THE 11 CONFEDERATE STATES:

Alabama, Arkansas, Florida, Georgia, Louisiana, Mississippi, North Carolina, South Carolina, Tennessee, Texas, Virginia.

- The Civil War began in 1861 when Confederate (southern) troops attacked Union (northern) troops at Fort Sumpter, in Charlestown harbor, South Carolina. The fighting didn't stop for four years.

- The northern states (the Union) had a much larger population than the 11 Confederate states of the South and a bigger army. Even so, the Confederate Army began the war by winning several major battles, led by tough-guy general Robert E. Lee.

- The Confederate Army's first big defeat was at the Battle of Gettysburg in 1863. By this time lots of African American soldiers were fighting for the Union, encouraged by President Lincoln's promise to end slavery. After that things started going a bit better for the Union.

- The Union general Ulysses S. Grant took control of the Confederate capital, Richmond, in 1865. Robert E. Lee surrendered, and soon after that the Civil War was over.

- The Civil War was extremely bloody. More American soldiers died in it than in the First and Second World Wars, and the Vietnam and Korean Wars all added together.

LEONIDAS

Leonidas was an ancient Greek king whose bravery in one battle made him famous for 2,500 years.

TOUGH
RATING: 7.5

SPARTAN LIFE

Leonidas was the son of King Anaxandrias II of Sparta. Sparta was an ancient Greek city-state that brought up its citizens to be fiercely patriotic. Leonidas wasn't heir to the throne so, like the sons of all Spartan citizens, Leonidas was sent to the *agoge*, a bit like an incredibly tough boarding school, at the age of seven. He became king after his half-brother died, around 490 BC.

PERSIAN INVASION

King Xerxes I, leader of the Persian Empire, tried to invade Greece in 490 BC but was defeated. Ten years later, he got together a massive army and navy and planned to make the whole of Greece part of the Persian Empire once and for all. Leonidas was put in charge of an alliance of Greek city-states, including Athens, to stop them at a pass between the mountains and the sea at a place called Thermopylae.

THE BATTLE OF THERMOPYLAE

Leonidas probably had around 7,000 men under his command. Unfortunately, the Persian King Xerxes had more than ten times that number. Leonidas defended the narrowest part of the pass. The Persians sent a message to Leonidas asking him to lay down his weapons. He replied, "Come and get them," in true tough-guy style. Massively outnumbered, the Greeks fought bravely and held back the Persians. But then a traitor told the Persians about

TOUGHOMETER

CUNNING: 7
COURAGE: 10
SURVIVAL SKILLS: 6
RUTHLESSNESS: 7

a path in the mountains so they could sneak behind the Greeks. Leonidas saw that this meant certain death. He sent most of the Greek army to safety, but bravely fought on with just 300 Spartan warriors. About 700 Thespians and 400 Thebans also stayed to help them fight. They delayed the Persians, but all of them died.

LEONIDAS THE HERO

Many Persian warriors were killed at Thermopylae. Xerxes was so angry about this that he had Leonidas's head cut off and his body crucified. This was unusual, because Persians usually treated opponents they deemed worthy with respect. The following year, the Greeks put a stop to Xerxes's invasion plans for good. Leonidas was celebrated as a hero, a shining example of fighting bravely against the odds and personal sacrifice for the good of his country.

Want to know what life was like in Sparta? See page 58.

LIVE LIKE A SPARTAN

BABY SPARTANS

Spartan babies were only allowed to live if they looked healthy—otherwise they were left to die. This was true of lots of other ancient civilizations too, so be glad you didn't live in those days.

BOARDING SCHOOL FOR THE TOUGHEST

Assuming you've survived and you want to grow up to be a Spartan citizen (in which case you need to be a boy—sorry, girls), you'll be sent away from your parents to a training school called the *agoge* when you're seven years old. You're divided into teams, and each team elects a leader—Sparta is a democracy, so this is a useful first lesson. By the way, you're not allowed to whinge.

WARRIOR TRAINING

If you're going to be a Spartan citizen, you're going to be a Spartan warrior (there's no choice about this). So you're trained to be at the peak of fitness, and you're taught how to fight. You'll also be expected to put up with quite a lot of physical pain. Without whingeing.

THIS DOES NOT LOOK GOOD...

SPARTAN COMFORTS

There aren't any comforts. You have to make your own bed from reeds picked from the river by hand. From the age of twelve the only item of clothing you're allowed is a cloak. You'll be given one of these a year—and you'd better be grateful for it. The most common food is black broth, made from pork, blood, and vinegar. As part of the training you won't always be given enough to eat, and will be encouraged to steal food using stealth and cunning. But if you're caught you'll be severely punished (this might be useful if you're ever stuck behind enemy lines).

GRADUATION

The *agoge* should turn you into a strong, fit, cunning, well-disciplined warrior. If you've done well in your training and passed all the tests, at the age of 20 you'll become a Spartan soldier, expected to fight in the army. You'll become a citizen when you're 30.

SPARTAN GIRLS

If you're a girl, your main responsibility in life is to produce good Spartan warriors. So girls have to make sure they're physically fit too, so that they have healthy babies— they learn dancing and sport. Girls are also taught to read and write, a skill most other Greek states don't bother teaching girls.

CHRISTOPHER COLUMBUS

Columbus made the most famous sea voyage in history, and opened up a whole "New World" for the Europeans.

COLUMBUS SETS SAIL

Christopher Columbus was born in Genoa, Italy, in 1451. When he grew up he became a sailor and settled in Portugal. The Europeans were very keen to find a new, less difficult route to Asia, where they traded for luxury goods like silk and spices. Like most educated people, Columbus knew the world was round, and he realized that if he could sail around the world to Asia and open up a new trade route, he would be rich and famous overnight.

THE WEST INDIES

He came up with charts for a route westward to Asia, and eventually King Ferdinand and Queen Isabella of Spain agreed to give him some ships and money. Columbus set sail in August 1492 with three ships, and by October he had reached the Bahamas, though he *thought* he'd reached Asia. He traveled on to Cuba and the island of Hispaniola, where he built a fort and left some of his men. He called the islands the West Indies and sailed back to Spain in ships laden with parrots, plants, gold, and a few of the friendly native islanders.

CUNNING: 6
COURAGE: 7
SURVIVAL SKILLS: 7
RUTHLESSNESS: 7

A SECOND VOYAGE

Everyone was impressed, and he was soon sent off on another voyage. Columbus returned to Hispaniola, only to discover that the locals had killed almost a quarter of the settlers he'd left behind on his first voyage. As punishment, Columbus demanded that each local over the age of 14 must deliver a gift of gold or cotton to the settlers every three months. If they failed, their hands were cut off and they were left to bleed to death.

TROUBLE IN PARADISE

A couple of years later Columbus set sail for a third time, exploring the Caribbean coast of South America (though he never set foot on North American land). But this time things didn't go so well. People in the Hispaniola colony had complained that Columbus had misled them about the riches to be found there, and Columbus was sent back to Spain a prisoner.

COLUMBUS'S LAST PORT

Eventually, Columbus was released and made another Atlantic voyage, but lost his ships and had to be rescued. He returned to Spain in 1504 and died 18 months later. He never found out that he hadn't reached Asia at all, but a completely different continent, which became known as the "New World."

THE EXPLORATION GAME

For two to six players. You'll need a token each and a die to play this game.

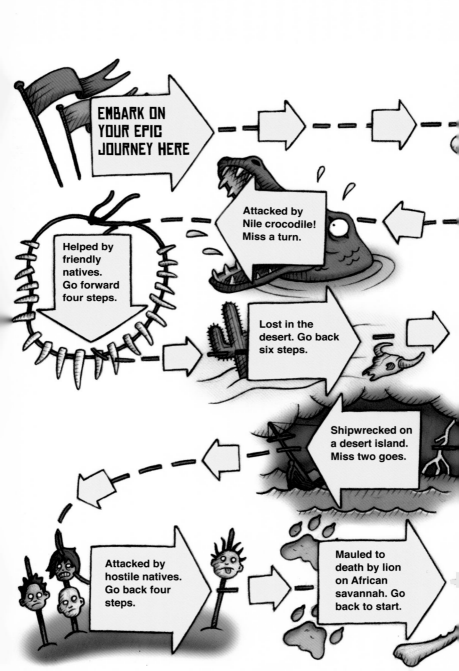

EMBARK ON YOUR EPIC JOURNEY HERE

Attacked by Nile crocodile! Miss a turn.

Helped by friendly natives. Go forward four steps.

Lost in the desert. Go back six steps.

Shipwrecked on a desert island. Miss two goes.

Attacked by hostile natives. Go back four steps.

Mauled to death by lion on African savannah. Go back to start.

Over the course of your travels as intrepid explorers, you voyage over sea and land into uncharted territory— dangerous jungles, arid deserts, the icy wastes of the Poles. Which of you will be the first to make it home? If you make it home at all…

Blown off course by unfavorable winds. Go back three steps.

Slip down icy crevasse in Antarctica. Miss a go.

Find an oasis. Go forward two steps.

Hit by poisoned dart in South American jungle. Miss a turn.

Favorable winds blow you toward home. Throw again.

Frostbite means you lose your toes! Take away two from every roll of the die from now on.

Bitten by venomous snake. Miss two goes.

TRIUMPHANT HOMECOMING!

AURANGZEB

Aurangzeb was the last of the great Mughal emperors in the 17th century, ruling over most of India and Pakistan. He made the Mughal Empire the biggest it had ever been.

TOUGH
RATING: 8.3

YOUNG AURANGZEB

Aurangzeb was born in 1618, the son of Mughal Emperor Shah Jahan and Mumtaz Mahal. (It was Shah Jahan who built the Taj Mahal as a memorial to his dead wife, Mumtaz). As a young man, Aurangzeb governed the Deccan (most of central and southern India), and later the Gujarat in north-west India, and led troops into Central Asia. He was ambitious, but his older brother was due to become emperor when Shah Jahan died.

CONQUEROR OF THE WORLD

When Emperor Shah Jahan became very ill in 1657 and it looked as though he might die, Aurangzeb and his older brother went to war. Aurangzeb defeated him, threw his father into prison (he had made a surprise recovery, and died in prison in 1666), and had both his brothers executed. He became emperor in 1658 and was crowned the following year, giving himself the modest title Alamgir, or "Conqueror of the World."

CONQUERING

Aurangzeb had a title to live up to. He fought off Persian and Central Asian invaders to the north of India and expanded the empire there. He also conquered new land in the center and south of India, making the empire the biggest it had ever been. He

TOUGHOMETER

CUNNING: 8
COURAGE: 8
SURVIVAL SKILLS: 7
RUTHLESSNESS: 10

had to besiege the city of Golconda for months, but it was worth it. When Golconda surrendered, Aurangzeb got his hands on the world's only diamond mine.

EVERYONE'S REVOLTING

The Muslim Mughals had been tolerant of the other main religion in India, Hinduism. But Aurangzeb taxed non-Muslims and destroyed Hindu temples. There were rebellions all over the place, especially in the areas he'd recently conquered, and Aurangzeb was constantly fighting to crush them. All the revolts were defeated, but all that fighting was expensive (even for someone with a diamond mine).

END OF AN EMPIRE

Aurangzeb ruled 150 million people. But after his death, aged 88, in 1707 the rebellions were successful, and the Mughal Empire didn't last long.

JULIUS CAESAR

Julius Caesar became the most important person in the whole of the ancient world. Then he got a bit *too* big-headed…

TOUGH
RATING: 8.3

CAESAR THE OUTLAW

Julius Caesar was born in 100 BC into a wealthy family in Rome. Rome was ruled by elected leaders called consuls, and had no king or queen. Caesar wanted a top job in politics but things started badly when Sulla, an old family enemy, came back to Rome from exile, seized power, and began executing thousands of his enemies. Caesar was made an outlaw and went into hiding, then joined the army and stayed away until Sulla died.

PIRATES!

On a trip to Greece, Caesar was captured by pirates and held to ransom. He was every bit as tough as the pirates and showed no fear of them at all. When the ransom had been paid, he sent ships to capture the pirates, and when they were caught he had them executed. He came back to Rome with a reputation for being brave and ruthless.

CAESAR INVADES

Caesar spent time and money showing off to important people (which was the only way to do well in ancient Roman politics), and landed a series of important jobs. As governor of Spain he invaded Portugal, killed lots of people, and stole loads of loot, which made him incredibly popular (in Rome, at least). He got the top job of consul, then took control of Rome with two buddies—Crassus (who defeated

TOUGHOMETER

CUNNING: 8
COURAGE: 9
SURVIVAL SKILLS: 7
RUTHLESSNESS: 9

Spartacus on page 21) and Pompey, an army general. Caesar started the Gallic Wars, in what's now France, which lasted for seven years and added modern France and Belgium to the Roman Empire.

CAESAR VS. POMPEY

After Crassus died, Pompey and Caesar went to war over who should be in charge of Rome. Caesar won. When he returned to Rome (after stopping off in Egypt where he fell in love with Queen Cleopatra), he was made Dictator of the Empire for ten years. But in 44 BC he went too far, he made himself Dictator for Life—just like a king. A month later 23 senators stabbed him to death.

Find out more about Cleopatra on page 82.

TOP TEN ROMAN EMPEROR FACTS

Caesar's death sparked a civil war that ended the Republic of Rome. After that Rome was ruled by emperors. Here are ten top facts about them, in order of when they ruled.

1. Augustus Octavian (ruled 27 BC–AD 14) was Julius Caesar's nephew. He called himself First Citizen rather than emperor, just in case everyone got upset and stabbed him to death.

2. Caligula (ruled 37–41) ordered his army to collect seashells and said he'd conquered the ocean. He also made senators run alongside his chariot, and thought of himself as a god.

3. As well as being a bit *eccentric,* Caligula was also extremely cruel. He had people murdered for their money and property. Eventually he was stabbed to death by his own bodyguards.

4. Claudius (ruled 41–54) died from being poisoned by his wife, Agrippina, who was also his niece.

5. Nero (ruled 54–68) was Claudius's stepson and Agrippina's son. Nero tried to kill his mother several times, and finally succeeded when he sent assassins to murder her.

6. Nero built an enormous grand house on the land cleared by a terrible fire in the city of Rome. He was suspected of starting the fire, so he accused the Christians of starting it instead, and had lots of them executed.

7. Commodus (ruled 180–192) fought as a gladiator against opponents whose weapons were made of lead so that he always won. He ended up being strangled by an assassin.

8. Elagabalus (ruled 218–222) liked to party but wasn't always good to his guests—he's supposed to have released thousands of rose petals from the ceiling on to his guests, suffocating them, and sometimes he let wild animals into guests' bedrooms while they were asleep. He was murdered by his own bodyguards, like Caligula.

9. Valerian (ruled 253–260) was captured by Shapur, leader of the Persians. Shapur killed him and had his body stuffed with straw and put on display.

10. Romulus Augustus (ruled 475–476) was the last emperor of the Western Roman Empire, and was probably between 10 and 14 years old when he took the throne. He was kicked out by the barbarian leader Odoacer less than a year later. But the Eastern Roman Empire, ruled from Constantinople, continued for ages.

QIN SHI HUANGDI

Qin Shi Huangdi united the whole of China and became its emperor. He also built the first Great Wall of China and an incredibly impressive tomb.

TOUGH
RATING: 7.8

KING OF QIN

Ying Zheng (who later became known as Qin Shi Huangdi) was born around 259 BC, the son of the king of the Chinese state of Qin. There were six other states in China at the time, and when Ying Zheng became king he decided he'd like to rule them all. From 230 BC he began conquering each of them and, nine years later, he'd managed it. In 221 BC he took the title Qin Shi Huangdi, which means "First Emperor."

EMPEROR

Qin Shi Huangdi decided to divide up the country so that the old regions no longer existed, and made the whole of China use the same coins, language, and weights and measures. He conquered even more land and expanded China to the south, into what's now Vietnam. He wasn't so successful in the north though. In fact, he got so fed up with northern invaders that he built a huge wall to keep them out—an early version of the Great Wall of China that exists today. Hundreds of thousands of workers, mostly captured enemies, built the wall—and at least seven out of every ten of them died from hunger and overwork.

TOUGHOMETER

CUNNING: 7
COURAGE: 7
SURVIVAL SKILLS: 8
RUTHLESSNESS: 9

To find out more about the history of ancient China, go to page 38.

MAGIC POTIONS AND FORBIDDEN BOOKS

According to later historians, Qin Shi Huangdi was desperate to find a potion to make him immortal. Not surprisingly, he didn't find one. But his disappointment led to him executing hundreds of people who thought his pursuit of magic was completely crazy. He also had very strict ideas about what jobs people should do and how they should behave—and if anyone didn't agree with him they might find themselves building the Great Wall of China. In 213 BC Qin Shi Huangdi ordered all books to be burned, unless they were about the Qin Empire, farming, medicine, astrology, or fortune telling— or unless they happened to be in his own library. He had hundreds of scholars buried alive for owning forbidden books.

THE TERRACOTTA ARMY

Qin Shi Huangdi died in 210 BC. He was buried in a massive underground tomb, guarded by thousands of life-size warriors and horses made from terracotta. It had taken tens of thousands of workers decades to build it. With Qin Shi Huangdi in his impressive grave, China only stayed united for another four years.

IVAR THE BONELESS

Ivar the Boneless was a fearsome Viking invader who conquered York and became an Irish king.

BONELESS AND HAIRYBREECHES

According to legend, Ivar was the son of Ragnar Hairybreeches, who had been thrown into a snake pit and killed by the Northumbrian King Aella. Lots of famous Vikings had nicknames (Skullsplitter or Snake-in-the-Eye, for example), but Ivar's is a puzzle, it doesn't sound very tough. It's been suggested that he was exceptionally bendy, but no one knows for sure.

IVAR'S INVASION

We do know that Ivar sailed to England from Denmark in 865 with two of his brothers and a large and terrifying army known as the Great Heathen Army—which probably consisted of hundreds of longships and thousands of men. The Vikings, the people of Norway, Sweden, and Denmark, had been raiding England for years, and had gained a very nasty reputation for killing and stealing anything they could find. Ivar had managed to build an even more terrifying reputation than most Vikings. He was supposed to be very tall, extremely wise, and *absolutely* ruthless.

THE VIKINGS HAVE COME TO STAY

TOUGHOMETER

CUNNING: 8
COURAGE: 8
SURVIVAL SKILLS: 8
RUTHLESSNESS: 10

Since around 850 the Vikings had not only been raiding England, but conquering bits of it. After Ivar and his brothers Halfdan and Ubbi landed and did a bit of pillaging and killing people, they decided to stay too. The following year, they embarked on a path of destruction and arrived in York, which they lost no time in conquering. While they were there, the brothers also killed King Aella—the one who had thrown their father into a snake pit—and got their revenge. According to later stories, this was the main reason for their visit to England.

IRISH IVAR

As well as invading England, the Vikings had also been busy invading Ireland. Before his expedition to conquer bits of England, Ivar the Boneless was joint King of Dublin. He returned to Ireland with hundreds of English prisoners, who were sent to the Viking slave markets in Dublin. Ivar's pillaging career ended in 873, when he died.

To find out more about Vikings and how tough they were, see page 74.

TOUGH VIKINGS

As a ruthless Viking marauder, Ivar the Boneless was far from alone. Here are some other Viking tough guys.

ERIC BLOODAXE lived in the tenth century. His father Harald Finehair was King of Norway, and Eric ruled after him. He's known as "Bloodaxe" probably because he murdered his brothers (there were lots of them, all wanting Harald's throne or some of his land or both). Later, he sailed to England, where he became King of Northumbria, but he made frequent visits to Scotland and Ireland to do a bit of pillaging.

RAGNAR HAIRYBREECHES was supposed to be the father of Ivar the Boneless and his brothers (who included Sigurd Snake-in-the-Eye and Björn Ironside). He's only known about from legends, so no one knows whether or not he really existed. The legend says that he got his nickname because he wore animal-skin pants while fighting a dragon, and he's supposed to have died when he was thrown into a snake pit by King Aella of Northumberland.

RAGNAR HAIRYBREECHES

ERIC THE RED left Norway with his father, who'd been sent into exile for killing someone, and settled in Iceland. Maybe Eric inherited his father's temper because, around 980, Eric ended up exiled from Iceland for killing someone in an argument too. Eric embarked on a dangerous 175-mile voyage to an unknown land he'd spotted from the highest mountains in Iceland. He called it Greenland, though it's not very green but extremely cold, icy, and inhospitable, and established a colony of Viking tough guys there.

LUCKY LEIF

LEIF ERICSON THE LUCKY was Eric the Red's son. He traveled even further than his father—he was probably the first European to set foot in North America (five centuries before Christopher Columbus). There are different accounts of Leif's voyages, but he was either blown off course on his way home to Greenland from Norway, or deliberately set out to find new lands. He probably landed on the Newfoundland coast, where archaeologists have discovered a Viking settlement. Later on a group of Vikings settled there, but eventually they were driven away by the Native Americans, who must have been *even* tougher than the Vikings.

To find out more about Christopher Columbus—who also sailed to America, go to page 60.

ABRAHAM LINCOLN

Abraham Lincoln is one of the most famous presidents ever. He succeeded in getting rid of slavery in America for good.

TOUGH
RATING: 6.3

YOUNG ABRAHAM

Abraham Lincoln was born in 1809 into a farming family in Kentucky. When he grew up he tried a few different jobs, then, despite having only been to school for less than a year altogether, he studied law books and became a lawyer when he was 27.

HEATED DEBATES

Lincoln was interested in the issue of abolishing slavery, which drew him into politics. He joined the Republican Party and challenged a Democrat for a seat in the Senate. He lost, but the debates he'd had with the Democrat about slavery made him famous—he'd had a lot of practice at persuasive speaking as a lawyer.

PRESIDENT LINCOLN

In 1860 Lincoln ran for election as President of the United States and won. The southern states were a bit alarmed by this, because Lincoln was anti-slavery and lots of people in the South wanted to keep slaves to work on plantations. So 11 southern (Confederate) states became independent from the rest of the Union. The year after Lincoln was elected the Civil War began.

CUNNING: 8
COURAGE: 8
SURVIVAL SKILLS: 6
RUTHLESSNESS: 3

EMANCIPATION PROCLAMATION

On new year's day in 1863, Lincoln issued the Emancipation Proclamation, which said that all slaves in southern states were free, and opened the Union Army to freed slaves. Every time

the northern states captured a region in the South, the slaves there were freed. About 180,000 of them joined the Union Army. Just before the Battle of Gettysburg, Lincoln gave an especially rousing speech reminding the Union troops of what they were fighting for: not only an end to slavery, but for a new kind of equality and freedom for all American citizens. The Union troops went on to win the most important victory of the war.

DEADLY ASSASSIN

The freed slaves helped win the Civil War. To celebrate, Lincoln went to the theater. Unfortunately, so did an assassin who supported slavery and wanted Lincoln dead. He shot him in the head and Lincoln died the next day. He's become known as the "Great Emancipator."

Find out more about the Civil War on page 54.

NAPOLEON BONAPARTE

Napoleon started out as an ordinary French soldier, but became an emperor with an army of hundreds of thousands of men.

NAPOLEON THE HERO

Napoleon Bonaparte was born in 1769 in Corsica. By 1789 he was an artillery officer in the south of France and a fierce supporter of the French Revolution, which had just begun. But not everyone supported the new government: there was a rebellion in Toulon, where foreign troops had landed to help the rebels. Napoleon led a brave attack, chased away the foreigners (including Nelson), and became an overnight hero.

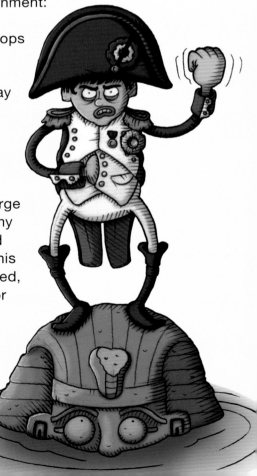

VICTORY AND DEFEAT

Napoleon was put in charge of leading the French Army against the Austrians and their allies. Even though his soldiers were badly clothed, underfed, and had inferior weapons, he defeated the Austrians easily. He wasn't so successful fighting the British in Egypt: Nelson sank Napoleon's ships and left him stuck there.

NAPOLEON TAKES CHARGE

When he finally got back to France Napoleon decided to sort things out by seizing power himself. In 1804 he made himself Emperor of France—rather like a king, even though the French had recently chopped their last king's head off.

INVASIONS

In an attempt to invade England, Napoleon's fleet was completely destroyed at the Battle of Trafalgar in 1805. Napoleon may have been defeated at sea, but on land he battered the Russians, Austrians, and Prussians. In 1812, he marched into Russia with 650,000 soldiers. The Russians didn't fight, but burned everything behind them so that the French had nothing to eat and nowhere to stay. Eventually the French retreated, exhausted, hungry, and freezing. The Russian Army now attacked them at their weakest. Only 40,000 men made it back to France.

END OF AN EMPIRE

France was forced to surrender and Napoleon was banished to the island of Elba. But as the old, unfair system of government returned, people started to miss Napoleon. In 1815 he marched to Paris and soon gathered an army—but eventually, at the Battle of Waterloo, they were beaten by the British forces. Napoleon was forced into exile on the island of Saint Helena in the South Atlantic, and died there in 1821.

MYSTERIOUS DEATH

Although an autopsy performed on Napoleon after his death reported that he died of stomach cancer, until recently, some scholars believed that he was deliberately killed by arsenic poisoning.

TOUGHOMETER

CUNNING: 8
COURAGE: 8
SURVIVAL SKILLS: 8
RUTHLESSNESS: 8

See page 80 to find out more about the French Revolution.

OFF WITH THEIR HEADS! THE FRENCH REVOLUTION

The French Revolution, one of the bloodiest in history, began after years of injustice by the French royals and nobles who were in power. The vast majority of the population lived in poverty but had to pay incredibly high taxes, while the rich lived in enormous houses, gallivanted in luxury but didn't have to pay _any_ taxes at all. Here's the short version of what happened.

1789 VIVE LA REVOLUTION! The peasants (the majority of France) are starving, and fed up with the unfair way their country is being governed. With the price of bread at an all-time high, they attack the Bastille prison in Paris, where weapons and ammunition are stored. This marks the beginning of the French Revolution. The revolutionaries take control of the government and pass new laws to make things fairer. Violence erupts against rich landowners all over France.

1791 ZUT ALORS! The French King Louis XVI is caught trying to escape revolutionary France.

1792 VIVE LA REPUBLIQUE! France is declared a republic. France is now at war with Austria, and soon lots of other countries too, including Britain, Spain, and the Netherlands. They want to make sure revolutions don't happen in their own countries (at least, the rich people do).

1793 LE TERROIR! King Louis XVI is executed by guillotine. Queen Marie Antoinette is executed the same way later that year. "The Terror" begins, led by a revolutionary called Robespierre, in which about 18,000 people who don't support the revolution are sent to the guillotine in one year.

1794 SACRE BLEU! The French people become fed up with Robespierre's passion for chopping off heads. Robespierre himself is arrested and guillotined and "The Terror" ends—or at least becomes a bit less terrible.

1795 LE DIRECTOIRE! Revolutionary France is now ruled by five directors, known as "the Directory."

1799 ZUT ALORS ENCORE! Napoleon overthrows the Directory and puts himself in charge.

1804 VIVE NAPOLEON! Napoleon becomes Emperor of France, despite an emperor being rather similar to a king, and the French people having beheaded their last king just over a decade earlier.

1815 FIN! Napoleon is defeated at the Battle of Waterloo and sent into exile. The victorious countries can't wait to get everything back to normal and put a king back on the throne. The brother of the beheaded King Louis is crowned king, and France lives under the reign of various kings and emperors for another 55 years.

NEXT!

ROBESPIERRE

CLEOPATRA

Cleopatra ruled Egypt and, with the help of some powerful boyfriends, might have ended up ruling Rome too.

PRINCESS CLEO

Cleopatra was born in 69 BC, the daughter of Egyptian ruler Ptolemy XII. Egypt had been ruled by a Greek royal family (the Ptolemies) since the death of Alexander the Great in 305 BC. Confusingly, almost all the men of the Ptolemy family were called Ptolemy, and almost all the women were called Cleopatra. When her father died, our Cleopatra became Cleopatra VII, joint ruler with her younger brother, Ptolemy XIII, whom she married (which was another one of the Ptolemys' strange habits). Cleopatra had to rule with her brother because the Egyptians didn't allow queens to rule on their own.

TROUBLE WITH PTOLEMY

Ptolemy was only about ten years old, but he wanted to get rid of his sister, so he and his supporters drove Cleopatra out of Egypt. In order to fight back, Cleopatra got help from one of the most powerful people in the world, Julius Caesar, who swiftly became her boyfriend. Together they defeated Ptolemy XIII, and Cleopatra was back in charge of Egypt. She ruled with a different brother this time, Ptolemy XIV.

TOUGHOMETER

CUNNING: 8
COURAGE: 8
SURVIVAL SKILLS: 7
RUTHLESSNESS: 8

CLEO AND CAESAR

Cleopatra spent most of her time in Rome with Caesar until he was assassinated in 44 BC. When she went back to Egypt, Ptolemy XIV was killed. Cleopatra probably had him poisoned so that she could rule with the baby son she'd had with Caesar, Caesarion.

CLEO AND MARK ANTONY

Mark Antony, one of the new Roman VIPs, asked Cleopatra for a meeting and promptly fell in love with her. The two of them stayed in Egypt together for a while, then Mark Antony returned to Rome. As part of a deal with Julius Caesar's heir, Augustus Octavian, Antony married Octavia, Octavian's sister, which must have annoyed Cleopatra.

DOUBLE DISASTER

After three years, Antony fell out with Octavian, abandoned his wife, and returned to Cleopatra. He declared that Caesarion should rule Rome because he was Caesar's son, so the Roman Senate declared war against Egypt. Octavian's ships met Antony and Cleopatra's at the Battle of Actium, which ended in disaster for Egypt. Antony went off to battle and heard that Cleopatra was dead (she wasn't), and stabbed himself with his own sword. After he died, Cleopatra killed herself. Legend has it that she let an asp (a venomous snake) bite her, and died of the poison.

Find out more about Cleopatra's famous boyfriend, Julius Caesar, on page 66.

SITTING BULL

Sitting Bull was a Native American warrior who fought to keep his people in their homeland.

TOUGH
RATING: 8

JUMPING BADGER

Sitting Bull was born around 1831, a member of the Teton Sioux tribe. He was named Jumping Badger, and only given his father's name, Sitting Bull, after his first battle with another tribe, the Crow tribe, when he was 14 years old.

THE SETTLERS ARRIVE

By the time Sitting Bull was 18, European settlers were moving westward through Sioux lands (what's now Montana, Nebraska, Wyoming, and North and South Dakota), especially after the California Gold Rush of 1849. There were frequent fights, in which Sitting Bull gained a reputation for bravery.

GOLD!

In 1866, Sitting Bull was made chief of the whole Sioux nation. In the mid 1870s, gold was discovered in the Black Hills of Dakota, where the Sioux lived. The government ordered the Native Americans to move into particular areas, called reservations, because they were getting in the way of the gold hunters. Sitting Bull didn't put up with it. He prepared to fight.

LITTLE BIGHORN

Sitting Bull gathered together the Sioux, Cheyenne, and some of the Arapaho tribes in the valley of the Little Bighorn River. In June 1876, Lieutenant Colonel Custer led his soldiers to their camp. Massively outnumbered by the Native Americans, Custer and *all* his men were killed.

TOUGHOMETER

CUNNING: 7
COURAGE: 9
SURVIVAL SKILLS: 8
RUTHLESSNESS: 8

EXILE

The U.S. army were so angry about what had happened to Custer that they forced many of the Sioux and other tribes to live on reservations. Sitting Bull led his people to Canada, where they lived a nomadic life hunting bison. But since the Europeans had arrived, the bison the Sioux depended on for food and hides had almost been wiped out. After four years, hunger drove Sitting Bull and his followers to surrender, and they went to live on a reservation. For a few months Sitting Bull joined *Buffalo Bill's Wild West Show*, a touring show that included displays of shooting and horse riding. Although he earned quite a lot of money by charging for autographs and photographs, he gave most of it away to beggars and the homeless.

SITTING BULL'S SAD END

In 1890, Native American police arrested Sitting Bull because they were worried that he might stir up trouble again. Over forty men were sent out to arrest him in a dawn raid. When Sitting Bull's followers found out what was happening, they started a fight. Sadly, the police retaliated by shooting Sitting Bull dead. He has become famous as a symbol of resistance.

Find out more about Native American tribes on page 86.

THE NATIVE AMERICAN TRIBE GUIDE

North America is very big, so there were lots of different groups of Native Americans living there before the European settlers arrived. Their way of life varied as dramatically as the landscape—from the icy tundra in Alaska to the swamps of Florida. Here's a brief guide to a few of them.

SIOUX

There were various groups of Sioux Native Americans— Sitting Bull was a member of the Hunkpapa division of the Teton Sioux tribe. They lived in teepees (a kind of tent made of animal skins and wooden poles) which they could move very quickly as they followed the herds of buffalo across the American plains. The Sioux were famous for their feathered war headdresses.

BEOTHUK

The Beothuk were the original people of Newfoundland in Canada. No one knows for sure, but it was probably the Beothuk who met the Vikings when they landed in North America. They lived in wigwams, cone-shaped wooden houses, and fished off the Newfoundland coast and hunted caribou and seals. They painted their bodies and clothing with red ochre. The last member of the Beothuk tribe died in 1829.

CHEROKEE

The Cherokee lived in the south-eastern states of Georgia, Tennessee, and western North and South Carolina (and some still do). They were farmers, living in small towns in log cabins. They traded with the settlers, adopted similar systems of government and customs, and helped the settlers to fight against other tribes. In 1838, after gold had been discovered in Georgia, tens of thousands of Cherokee Native Americans were

GERONIMO

forced from their homes and marched over 800 miles to Oklahoma. Thousands of them died on the way. The march became known as the "Trail of Tears."

APACHE

The Apache lived in the south-western states of Colorado, New Mexico, and Texas, and today they live in Oklahoma and New Mexico. There are Western and Eastern Apache tribes, each with different divisions. In the past the Apache farmed and hunted, and lived in small brush shelters or wooden-framed tents. They were one of the fiercest Indian tribes, resisting colonization by the Spanish settlers from South America and the European settlers from the North. Geronimo, who fought against both the Mexicans and the U.S. army, was one of the most famous Apache warriors. It's said he was so tough that he attacked a group of Mexican soldiers armed with only a knife, even though the soldiers were armed with guns.

 Find out more about when Vikings met the Beothuk on page 74.

GRACE O'MALLEY

Grace O'Malley defied convention to become wealthy and powerful, and one of the most feared pirates of her time.

TOUGH
RATING 8.3

THE O'MALLEY CLAN

Grace O'Malley was born around 1530 in south-west County Mayo, Ireland, surrounded by mountains and the sea, the daughter of the O'Malley chieftain. The O'Malleys were seafaring people who traded with France, Spain, and Portugal, with a bit of piracy on the side.

BALD GRACE

Legend has it that when Grace was about eleven, she wanted to go on a trading voyage to Spain with her father, but she was told her long hair would catch in the ropes. So she cut it all off—and got the nickname "Bald Grace." She probably learned seafaring, trading, and, of course, piracy from her father.

SETTING SAIL

Grace began her own trading business when she grew up, even though it was an extremely unusual thing for a woman to do. When her first husband, Donal O'Flaherty, died in the early 1560s, Grace moved back to her childhood home of Clare Island. The O'Flaherty men were so loyal to her that many of them followed her.

TOUGHOMETER

CUNNING: 8
COURAGE: 8
SURVIVAL SKILLS: 9
RUTHLESSNESS: 8

PLUNDER ON THE HIGH SEAS

Grace O'Malley's ships would stop traders sailing into Galway and other Irish ports, and demand goods or cash from them in return for a safe passage. If the traders refused, their ship would be plundered.

AMAZING GRACE

Grace gained a reputation for bravery and cunning. According to one story, she was besieged in one of her castles by the English (who were supposed to be in control of Ireland and were fed up with Grace's piracy) with very few men. Grace ordered the men to take the lead off the roof and melt it, then she poured it on the attacking soldiers' heads. The English fled, giving Grace time to rally support before beating them soundly in battle.

TWO QUEENS

English power in Ireland grew, and things became more and more difficult for Grace. In 1593, she met with Queen Elizabeth I in London, to ask for the release of her sons and half-brother, who had been imprisoned by the English governor of Connaught. Grace continued her life of piracy. She died around 1603, but lives on in songs and legends.

Find out about another famous pirate, Blackbeard, on page 8.

SCOTT OF THE ANTARCTIC

TOUGH
RATING: 6.5

Explorer and British naval officer Scott led two daring and dangerous expeditions to the most inhospitable place on Earth. His bravery made him a national hero.

SCOTT SETS SAIL

Robert Falcon Scott was born in Plymouth, south-west England, in 1868. He joined the British Navy as a cadet when he was 13 and served on ships all around the world. But he made his name as an explorer, not as a sailor.

A CHILLY EXPEDITION

Scott was chosen to lead an expedition to the Antarctic, despite the fact that he knew very little about being an explorer, or the South Pole. He set off, in command of his ship *Discovery*, in 1901. Three years later, the expedition returned: they had survived the coldest place on Earth (the lowest temperature in the world was recorded there: -129° Farenheit) and the disease scurvy (caused by not enough vitamin C). But they hadn't made it to the South Pole.

THE ANTARCTIC AGAIN

In 1910, Scott sailed for the Antarctic on an expedition to be the first to reach the South Pole. The following year he set off over the icy land with eleven other men. Things didn't start well: half their ponies died and the dog teams were sent back, and the men had to haul their own sleds across the ice. Seven men were sent back to base camp, while Scott and the other

TOUGHOMETER

CUNNING: 4
COURAGE: 10
SURVIVAL SKILLS: 9
RUTHLESSNESS: 3

four carried on. After months of battling blizzards, they arrived at the South Pole only to discover that their rival, the Norwegian Roald Amundsen, had got there a month before.

BACK TO BASE

Scott and his team turned towards base camp, 800 miles away. They struck terrible weather. Soon, one man, Edgar Evans, died. Another man, Lawrence Oates, got frostbite in his hands and feet—he didn't want to hold back the others and sacrificed himself by walking off into a blizzard. The other three men, including Scott, all died of cold and hunger only a day's walk from more supplies. Their bodies were found months later.

Roald was 'ere

TOKUGAWA IEYASU

Tokugawa Ieyasu was a Samurai warrior who became Shogun (leader) of all Japan. His descendants ruled for hundreds of years.

A DIFFICULT CHILDHOOD

Tokugawa Ieyasu was born in 1543, during the Era of Warring States, the son of a Samurai warrior. His family were split between supporting two different warring clans, the Imagawa and the Oda. Ieyasu's father preferred the Imagawa. When the Oda invaded Ieyasu's hometown, his father sent his son to live with the Imagawa in return for their help in fighting off the Oda. But on the way he was kidnapped by the Oda clan. Ieyasu was only five at the time. Two years later, the Oda gave Ieyasu to the Imagawa, where he was raised, trained, and fought as a warrior.

A BIT OF BASHING

In 1560, the Imagawa clan chief was killed in a battle with Oda Nobunaga and Ieyasu, now aged 17, returned to his family's small castle. He switched his loyalties and allied himself to Oda Nobunaga, and gradually expanded his domain by leading war parties against his neighbors. By the 1580s he was an important baron.

BAD PARENTING

In 1579, Ieyasu's eldest son was accused of plotting against his father. As punishment (and possibly with some persuasion from Oda Nobunaga), Ieyasu ordered his son to commit suicide, and had his son's wife executed.

TOUGHOMETER

CUNNING: 10
COURAGE: 10
SURVIVAL SKILLS: 10
RUTHLESSNESS: 10

MORE BASHING

In 1582, Oda Nobunaga killed himself because he'd been wounded by someone less important than him (this was the kind of thing expected of a Samurai). His general, Hideyoshi, took his place. Ieyasu and Hideyoshi together organized an army and navy and took control of new lands. Ieyasu now had lots of new territory, which he looked after and defended carefully. When he wasn't waging war or ordering people to kill themselves, he enjoyed swimming and falconry.

BATTLE OF SEKIGAHARA

Hideyoshi died in 1598 and there was a struggle among the Samurai lords to take his place. Ieyasu had the biggest army in the whole of Japan. In 1600, he won the Battle of Sekigahara and was now in control of most of the country. In 1603 he was made Shogun, the most powerful general in Japan. After only two years he retired and made his son Shogun in his place, but really he was still running things from behind the scenes.

A WARRIOR'S LEGACY

When he died at the age of 73, Ieyasu's castle at Edo was the biggest in the world, and he'd brought an end to the Era of Warring States. Ieyasu's descendants went on to rule Japan for another 250 years.

THE SAMURAI AND THEIR WEAPONS

The first Samurai were bodyguards for Japanese lords, but eventually they became a noble warrior class, famous for their toughness and their warrior code, "Bushido," which stressed loyalty, honor, self-discipline, and respect. During the Era of Warring States in the 1400s and 1500s, Japan was split into lots of different territories, which were constantly at war. After Tokugawa Ieyasu united Japan in 1603, things were much more peaceful.

THE WAY OF THE WARRIOR

Samurai are some of the most terrifying warriors in history, with their elaborate and scary armor. They also had some mean weapons:

SWORD: the most famous Samurai weapon—long (more than 23 inches) and curved, with a large, often elaborately decorated hilt. Samurai often carried two swords—a long one and a shorter one (just in case), with the two hilts sticking out of the front of their armor menacingly.

TESSEN: an iron fan—the kind you can open and cool yourself down with. But the main reason Samurai carried tessens was because they were extremely useful for bashing people over the head, but didn't count as weapons. That way, even if a warrior had to hand over all his weapons, he'd never really be unarmed.

MANRIKIGUSARI: a yard-length metal chain, with handles at either end. In skilled hands the manrikigusari was an accurate and often deadly weapon. Its name means "the strength of a thousand men."

JUTTE: a huge metal truncheon for deflecting sword thrusts, disarming an opponent, and, of course, bashing people over the head.

SHAKUHACHI: the shakuhachi, or bamboo flute, was originally just a musical instrument. Later, shakuhachis were made bigger and heavier so that they could be used as weapons—with the added bonus that warriors could play themselves a lovely tune after a fight.

As if these weren't enough, Samurai had other weapons they might use: a long bow called a yumi, and, from the sixteenth century, firearms and cannons.

HOW TOUGH ARE YOU?

These questions are based on the lives of some of the people in this book. Choose your answers, and find out if you've got what it takes to be one of history's toughest! Work out your score on page 99.

1. You are imprisoned in a gladiatorial school, being trained to fight to the death. Do you...

a) Start planning a slave rebellion that will bring Rome to its knees.

b) Hatch an escape plan—after the escape you'll run away to safety.

c) Train as hard as you can so that you can live as long as possible—you might be granted your freedom one day.

d) Hide and hope no one will notice.

2. You're a French farmer's daughter living in a village in a part of France under English control. Do you...

a) Do nothing—you're just a farmer's daughter after all.

b) Grumble a lot about the evil English.

c) Talk to the villagers and try to start a rebellion.

d) Demand an audience with the king, convince him to put you at the head of an army, and lead it to victory against the English.

3. Out riding your horse one day on the Mongolian Steppes, you spot a village in the distance. Do you...

a) Stop by for a chat and a glass of lemonade.

b) Chuckle evilly and plan an attack with your conquering hordes.

c) Gallop away in fear of hostile locals.

d) Post guards to keep an eye on the villagers in case they threaten your lands.

4. You're an Egyptian leader with a history of powerful Roman boyfriends. But now it looks as though some other Romans have defeated you in battle. Do you...

a) Have a meeting with the

victorious Roman leader—maybe you should get to know one another better?

b) Load as much of your enormous wealth as possible on to a barge and sail off into the sunset.

c) Accept defeat—but be very grumpy about it.

d) Kill yourself with a venomous asp.

5. You are a Victorian woman of means whose parents have recently died. Do you...

a) Put your feet up and enjoy an easy life.

b) Spend a lot of your time working for charities.

c) Become a nurse.

d) Explore uncharted regions of Africa, climb mountains, meet cannibalistic tribes, and survive an attack by a crocodile.

6. You are commanding a ship during a naval battle. One of your arms is hit by a musket and badly damaged. Do you . . .

a) Ask for it to be amputated as soon as possible. Get back to commanding your officers within 30 minutes of the operation.

b) Faint.

c) Put someone else in charge and take to your bed to recover.

d) Climb the rigging to escape the surgeon.

7. Which is your gladiatorial weapon of choice?

a) The trident, dagger, and net of the Retiarius. It looks real tough.

b) The Sagittarius's bow and arrow. You have a deadly aim.

c) A sword and shield. Can the shield be really, really big?

d) Choice of weapons is irrelevant—you would win armed only with your bare hands!

8. The Romans have invaded and their army is rapidly approaching. Do you...

a) Do nothing. You've heard the Romans aren't that bad, and let you keep your own religion and stuff.

b) Amass an army of fierce tribesmen. You're going down fighting.

c) Arrange a meeting with their leader.

d) Move further north. You fancy a change anyway.

9. In a Viking battle...

a) You arm yourself with an enormous battle ax and leap in.

b) You make strategic battle plans from a safe distance.

c) You dress in a bearskin and work yourself into a frenzy biting your sword and howling, believing you have superhuman powers and the protection of Odin.

d) You take one look at the berserkers (warriors) and run away.

10. You're a Norman conqueror who needs to defeat the rebels in the North of England. You decide to . . .

a) Send a small force with a list of strongly worded demands.

b) Hope they come round in the end.

c) Meet the rebels in fierce battle.

d) Kill everyone in the North, destroy all the crops, and set fire to everything.

SCORE AS FOLLOWS FOR YOUR ANSWERS:

1. a) 10; b) 3; c) 7; d) 0

2. a) 0; b) 3; c) 7; d) 10

3. a) 3; b) 10; c) 0; d) 7

4. a) 7; b) 0; c) 3; d) 10

5. a) 0; b) 3; c) 7; d) 10

6. a) 10; b) 3; c) 7; d) 0

7. a) 3; b) 7; c) 0; d) 10

8. a) 3; b) 10; c) 7; d) 0

9. a) 7; b) 3; c) 10; d) 0

10. a) 3; b) 0; c) 7; d) 10

NOW ADD UP YOUR SCORES:

70–100

Congratulations. You're one tough cookie. Consider world domination as a career.

50–69

You can be tough, but you're not quite tough enough. Still, most people would be glad to have you on their team. Good effort.

25–49

You're way too soft for risk-taking or stirring up trouble. Must try harder.

0–24

Let's face it, you're a total wimp. Why not pick some flowers, or stroke a bunny rabbit, or something?

HISTORY'S TOUGHEST TIMELINE

480 BC

Spartan King Leonidas died defending a narrow pass (a path through the mountains) at the Battle of Thermopylae. He was leading the united Greek city-states in a battle against the Persians.

356 BC

Alexander the Great, King of Macedonia, was born. The vast empire he conquered included the whole of Greece.

259 BC

Qin Shi Huangdi was born around this date. He united the warring states of China and became the "First Emperor" of China.

109 BC

Spartacus, the Roman gladiator who led a huge slave revolt, was born around this date.

100 BC

Julius Caesar was born. He became too powerful and upset the ancient Roman senators—who murdered him in 44 BC.

69 BC

Egyptian Queen Cleopatra was born. She had two powerful Roman boyfriends, including Julius Caesar, but was defeated by the future First Citizen of Rome, Augustus Octavian.

AD 43

The Romans invaded Britain and conquered much of the South. Roman rule would last over 350 years.

30

Boudicca, queen of the British Iceni tribe, was born around this date. She fought the Romans ferociously until she was defeated at the Battle of Watling Street.

453

Barbarian leader Attila the Hun died, after a lifetime on the rampage. Soon after, the Western Roman Empire fell and the Dark Ages began in Europe.

500

Around the year 500, the Huns destroyed the Gupta Empire in northern India.

624

Chinese Empress Wu Zetian was born. She started out as one of the emperor's many concubines (a kind of second-class wife), but became the only empress ever to rule China.

742

Charlemagne, the King of the Franks, was born. He battered the Saxons and the Lombards (among others), and was crowned the First Emperor of what became known as the Holy Roman Empire.

CHARLEMAGNE

HISTORY'S TOUGHEST TIMELINE

873

Ivar the Boneless, fearsome Viking warrior and king, died around this date, having spent his life pillaging England and Ireland. Meanwhile, the huge and highly cultured Islamic Empire included Spain, North Africa, Persia (Iran), and Syria.

1028

William the Conqueror was born around this date. The Norman Duke conquered England after one of the most famous battles in English history, the Battle of Hastings in 1066. Sixty or so years before, Viking Leif Ericson had made his first voyage to North America.

1162

Genghis Khan, conqueror and ruler of the vast Mongol Empire, was born around this date. Meanwhile, the Native American Anasazi people were building cliff dwellings in the American south-west.

1305

William Wallace, who fought to kick the English out of Scotland, died in 1305. He was hanged, drawn, and quartered by English King Edward I. Around 50 years later, the Black Death was at its worst, killing millions throughout Europe.

1412

Joan of Arc, the young girl who led the French army to victory against the English, was born around this date.

1451

Christopher Columbus was born. After he landed in the West Indies in 1492, lots of Europeans followed. Soon after, the Spanish conquered the Aztec Empire in Central America, and the Incan Empire in South America. Also around this time, the printing press was invented.

1530

Ivan the Terrible, the first ruler of the whole of Russia, was born. In the same year, or thereabouts, Grace O'Malley, the fearsome Irish pirate queen, was born. Also in the same year, the first Mughal Emperor, Babur, died (he was a descendant of Genghis Khan, and Aurangzeb's great, great, great grandfather).

1543

Samurai warrior Tokugawa Ieyasu was born. He became Shogun (leader) of all Japan and brought peace to the country (but only after a lot of violence).

1618

Aurangzeb, the last Mughal Emperor, was born. Not long afterward, the Pilgrim Fathers sailed to America aboard the *Mayflower* and became the second successful English colony in North America.

JOAN OF ARC

HISTORY'S TOUGHEST TIMELINE

1680

Notorious pirate Blackbeard was born around this date. He plundered the seas off the coast of North America, which had been settled by Europeans since 1565.

1758

English naval hero Lord Nelson was born. He grew up to defeat Napoleon at the Battle of Trafalgar.

1769

Napoleon, French general and eventually Emperor of France, was born, and expanded the lands of Revolutionary France. Meanwhile Captain Cook was making maps of Australia and New Zealand, and colonies in America fought the Revolutionary War to become the United States of America.

1809

Abraham Lincoln, the President of the United States who abolished slavery, was born.

1820

Fearless ex-slave and Underground Railroad conductor, Harriet Tubman, was born around this date. The slave trade had been made illegal in Britain 13 years previously, but despite this, slavery was allowed to continue in the United States, the British Empire, and many other parts of the world.

1822

Ulysses S. Grant was born, Union general in the bloody Civil War. Meanwhile the Industrial Revolution was well under way, changing the way people lived and worked forever.

1831

Sitting Bull was born, leader of the Sioux Native Americans who fought against settlers to keep the Sioux in their homeland. Slavery was abolished in the British Empire two years later.

1862

Mary Kingsley, intrepid Victorian explorer, was born. Three years later, slavery was abolished in the United States.

1868

English navy officer and explorer, Scott of the Antarctic, was born. Two years after his death near the South Pole, the First World War began in 1914, which killed more than 15 million people.

1948

Gandhi, who led peaceful protests to make India independent from Britain, was assassinated. He died in the middle of a century that saw revolutions in China, Russia, Mexico, and other countries, and two World Wars.

BABY BLACKBEARD

GLOSSARY

ABOLISH   To officially end an activity or custom

AD   All dates after the year that Jesus was born, also known as CE (the Common Era)

ASSASSIN   Someone who kills a famous or important person, often for political reasons or for money

BANISH   Send someone away and forbid them to come back

BARBARIAN   Person from a different country or culture that is thought to be more violent than your own

BC   All dates before the year that Jesus was born, also known as BCE (Before the Common Era)

BESIEGE   Surround a place with armed forces

BLOCKADE   Seal or block off a place to stop goods or people from entering or leaving

BOWSPRIT   Pole sticking out from the front (bow) of a ship

BOYCOTT   To refuse to buy a certain product or use a certain service as a form of protest

BREECHES   Trousers that stop just below the knee

BRIGADIER GENERAL   Officer in the U.S. army above colonel and below major general

CADET   Young trainee in the military or police

CENTURION   Officer in the Roman Army who was in charge of 100 soldiers

CHIEFTAIN   Leader of a tribe

CIVIL WAR   War between people who live in the same country

CONSUL   Person chosen to live in a foreign place who takes care of visitors from their own country

COMMODORE   Important officer in the navy

DICTATOR   Ruler with total power over a country

DOWRY Money or property which a woman's parents give to the man she marries

DYNASTY Period of time where all the rulers or leaders come from the same family

ECCENTRIC Out of the ordinary or strange

EMANCIPATION Giving people social or political freedom and rights

EMPIRE Group of countries ruled by a single person, government, or country

EXILE To be sent or kept away from your own country or village

FALCONRY Sport of hunting small animals and birds using falcons

FIRST MATE Officer on a ship who is second in charge to the captain

GLADIATOR Person trained to fight for entertainment

GUILLOTINE Machine for cutting people's heads off

HIDE Animal skin

HILT Handle of a sharp, pointed weapon such as a sword

IMMORTAL Living or lasting forever

INVADE Enter a country or city in order to take over or cause damage

LEGION A group of 3,000–6,000 men in the ancient Roman Army

LONGSHIP Wooden ships made and used by the Vikings

LOOT Stolen money or goods

MARAUDER Person that goes from one place to another looking for something to kill or steal

MOORISH Word to describe Muslims who came from Africa and conquered most of Spain and Portugal in AD 711

NOMADIC Lifestyle where people move from place to place

OCHRE A yellowish-orange kind of clay

OUTLAW Person who is not protected by law

OVERLORD Ruler

PAGAN Person who has religious beliefs that do not belong to the main world religions

PILLAGE Steal something from a place or a person using violence

PLANTATION Area of land on which crops such as coffee, sugar, cotton, and tobacco are grown

PLUNDER Steal cargo, money, or belongings

PRIVATEER SHIP Ship that is officially allowed to attack foreign ships during wartime

REPUBLIC Country without a monarch (king or queen) in charge

SCHOLAR Person who studies a subject in great detail

SENATOR Politician who has been elected

SETTLEMENT Place a group of people have made their home

SLAVE Person who is the legal property of another person

TANNER Person who turns animal skins into leather

TAPESTRY Cloth with an embroidered picture on it that often tells a story

TEEPEE Type of tent in the shape of a cone made from animal skins and wooden poles

TERRACOTTA Baked reddish-brown clay

TRIBE Group of people who live together

UPRISING Act of resistance or rebellion

WEEVIL Small beetle that lives in stored food

WIGWAM Dome-shaped living space made of wood covered with canvas, animal skins, or grass

INDEX